Elite Point Fighting and the Meaning of Life

By

Darius P. Prewitt

To a good
friend and
great brother
C.B. '86!!

Darius P. Prewitt

ISBN: 9798780243687

Table of Contents

Forward

Before I get started with this book, let me go over a few critical things. This book talks about two things. Competitive point fighters and finding out what the meaning of life is. The latter is harder but can be discovered by doing the former. The goal of this book is to make both easier for you to discover and therefore accomplish.

This book is also a conversation between you, the reader, and me the writer. The language is intentionally informal. This is not an academic piece. I want us to speak to one another and talk about how to be better at what we do. This book is meant to impart advise and consult you on how to be better at fighting. Let us start by looking at martial types of martial artist.

First, the martial arts are comprised of three types of people and they are warriors, fighters, and competitors. All are students. A very small number of people are a mix of the three. Most are a combination of two and the rest are just one. This book is referring to the latter.

Martial arts, no matter the style, country, or era, always have two components. Yes, some have more than that or will be in denial about or express it in different fashions, but at the core, I swear on my daughter's dreadlocks and my wife's famous banana pudding, there are two clear and obvious parts to all martial arts.

They may not be evident at first or even apparent to the novice, but they are always there. The instructor, coach, trainer, drill sergeant, or whoever it is teaching it may not say it first, but all fighting styles will have a competitive part and a self-defense part. Why this is, is primal but relatively easy to explain.

First, self-defense is the main reason for training in martial arts. It is the "raison d'etre" for combat. Achilles, Masomoto, Patton, Ali, and little Mulan, all want to defend themselves. However, once they are at a certain level, they want to prove that it's not just luck. This is when and where competition comes into play. Once we reach the game realm, the philosophy, and benefits from it comes into sharp focus and are in plain view. To demonstrate this, let's look at western boxing.

Boxing is called the sweet science. The science part of it is because fighters are thinkers. They strategize. In combat, as in war, they are tough and must make decisive decisions. Many think of boxing as an art. Its canvas is the ring and the face or body of the opponent. Competition helps to test and validate the training and skill of the artist. It also acts as the lenses through which we view the art. We leave the battlefield's savagery and move it to the more theatrical venue of the mat, ring, cage, or octagon.

The percentage of how much they are trained on each will vary wildly. I would prefer that it was 75% self-defense and 25% competition, but that is not the case in most places globally, but especially the most commercial schools open to the public. Most businesses have 85% competition and 15% self-defense. Why is it that way? The competition pays the bills.

Martial arts, no matter the style or country of origin, have one goal, kick the other person's butt. It does not matter if it is on the street or in the ring. Suppose you, the fighter, can come back and say that you can or did defeat an opponent. In that case, that is good enough, but what is better is that you have trophies and medals that you can display at home, in your windows or on various websites, that if honorable and true, demonstrate that you did defeat an opponent(s).

In the ancient world in Europe and Asia (to be honest almost any place on the planet), fighters who have gone against advanced fighters, would either be thrown into an arena, pit or some other public venue to do battle. They would fight and be judged as to if they were competent or not. Usually this meant that they would live or die. Luckily, we are far more enlightened and always allow our fighters to live.

Fighting is a little different than other sports. The barebones thing about fighting competitively is that you want to be there. Self-defense is different. You don't want to be there. Life has just put you in a lousy situation and now you are forced to fight. Stuff happens and you must deal with it.

In competition you WANT to be there. Life did not put you in this situation, you did. You choose this and because you choose this it's time that you take this seriously. Fighters of all types (point, full contact, mma, tae kwon do, judo, pancreas, boxing, savate or street fighting) have a particular primal view and philosophy.

If we fight, in competition and the street, only one of us will win and it will be me. Fighting is primal and has primal reactions to challenge. If you hurt my family or friends, you can kiss it goodbye. If you disrespect me or take me as a joke, I will destroy you. If you come halfway or think of me as a joke, I will bring the pain and make you suffer for it. I am the boogeyman under the bed. I am the monster in the closet. I am your worst nightmare. These reactions are natural and apply to fighting, business, and other forms of competition.

As you may have guessed, fighting involves big heaping mounds of pain and discomfort. Not just for your opponent, but in the training to beat your foe. You are intentionally giving people the opportunity to punch and kick you until someone, not you, says stop. You train to make the pain go away or become marginally acceptable.

The whole purpose of this book is to get you ready for this little party and get you to the point so that you can do it to the best of your abilities. You should take this as seriously as you possibly can. If you take this seriously and listen to your team and a little bit to me, you will, maybe, have only a few bruises. With that you can brag about those bruises and not try to hide when you go back to your office during the first day after your competition.

If you stay at this for more than just a little while, likely, it is possible and maybe even likely, that you will acquire a few broken bones, pulled or torn tendons, get wrestlers/cauliflower ear (it's worse than it sounds), have a cracked rib or two and break at least one toe. I do not want to disgust you with talk of abrasions or lacerations, they are just part of the normal training routine, but they are what will happen to you if you continue to read this book and decide you want to fight.

Like in everything else in life, people fight for different reasons. Some just want to see if they can do it. A good buddy of mine just wanted to know if he could take a punch. I wanted to prove to my friends that I was as tough as they were. Whatever your reason, it's yours, but that reason must be strong enough to make sure that you are going to do whatever it takes to train hard and consistently, so that your reason continues to make sense to you.

With fighting you don't want to be just okay. Okay makes you lose teeth and breaks your bones. Whatever your reason is, it's going to talk to you when you are at that bus stop or in the car driving to the gym. Make sure that you can accept and continue to listen to that reason every day that you train and before you fight every opponent you meet.

I am not some world champion. I have a few minor trophies and medals. There are those with far more accolades and praises then I do. What separates me from some, is my love and admiration for the greats. I am a student of the arts. I love the minutia and study of martial arts. I could sit in a corner with a fighter and talk to them for hours about what and how they do what they do. For 47 years I have studied, fought, sparred, talked, and listened to the kings and queens of sport karate and beyond. This is only part of what I have learned.

Now on with our show…...

Introduction

This book is about fighting. Period. Yes, the title says that it is about point fighting specifically, but it is about fighting in general, and on a more microscopic level about fighting that has its roots in Southeast Asia. I will go into things that some books only marginally talk about or just ignore completely.

Things such as philosophy, psychology, the strategy of fighting, science of fighting and what to do to make you better at it. Most of this is based on my direct experience as a point fighter, street fighter, teacher, coach, and enthusiast. This is not a step-by-step book. It's a book about the process. Having said that, there will be some step-by-step things that we will go over. In the fighting technique chapter.

What will make this different is that the pictures and techniques will have direct links to YouTube videos that correspond directly to what is in the books. We will switch up videos as we find new ones that make our points or are better than what we had prior. Periodically we will have updates and changes. Hopefully, this will happen organically in response to what our readers and fighters have found to work for them. This last part is very important, because the goal of this book is to provide practical battle tested information for everyone that reads it.

Throughout history, there have been several common keys to success for all fighters. It's not rocket science, but it does take perseverance, discipline, consistency, and dedication. These three things are key to the success of anyone in anything, but especially so with fighting. Without perseverance, discipline, and dedication you are bound to fail. It's inevitable. The keys to success in fighting are common sense things, but without perseverance, dedication, and discipline, you will fail.

This book is for both the beginner and the experienced fighter. We will discuss a wide range of things, but certain things we will talk about repeatedly. They are foundational to the development of a fighter. Coaches, sensei's, instructors, and fighters talk about these key components all the time. They do so because they help to create fighters who are winners.

Those components are diet, conditioning, exercise, technique, and psychology. These are the five things that all fighters have who not only survive, but who wins. In competition, winning is the only thing that matters. In the art, it's only part of what you achieve.

The first thing that manifests your understanding of these key ideas is the hardest and probably makes the least sense. Diet. If you cannot control what you put in your body and manage your food, you will lose every time. Not just in fighting but in any endeavor, you strive at. It is the cornerstone of any fighting champions foundation of success.

This is going to make some people angry, but unless you have been diagnosed with a genetic or biological defect, there really is not a good reason for you to be fat. This is anathema to any championship level fighter. If you are eating lots of fatty, greasy food and drinking sugary drinks day in and day out and no one is forcing you to AND you have alternatives available to you, you are lazy and you are going to be fat. Next up is conditioning.

Exercise is nothing without conditioning for a fighter and yes exercise and conditioning are two different things. Conditioning is the thing that gets you ready mentally and physically due to intensity. Exercise is about direct resistance and physical strength. Conditioning is layered and more about increasing your determination. A well-conditioned fighter is usually a more adaptable fighter. Just as it is in biological evolution it is in fighting. The more adaptable you are, the more likely you are not only to survive but to conquer.

Now we have exercise. When you were little you probably heard people talk about you growing up to be big and strong. Being big can be cool but being strong is better. Exercise makes you strong. Hard challenging exercise makes your muscles stronger. It is what gives you physical power.

Next up is technique. Good technique in a fit body can save your life and lead you to victory. Good technique is nothing more than muscle memory. You practice over and over and over until the body learns a particular movement. Once the body knows it, the fighter doesn't have to think about it. It's there and will come when needed. Grapplers live by this. However, the technique is a very small but important part of a fighter's development. How your fist, feet, elbows, knees move through the air to your opponent comes from the why and the how of what your intentions are. For the competitor this comes from strategic planning.

We also have the psychological components. These are the things that allow you to have the confidence to persevere and defeat your opponent even when you doubted yourself. Learning good ring/mat strategy and management will give you an insurmountable edge over your competition from a mental standpoint. The great fighters can physically dominate but also psychologically control the people that they fight. This and all the other foundational components will be talked about repeatedly throughout this book.

Why Buy This Book

Why should you purchase this book? If you are a fighter and you buy this book you probably fall into one of three categories. Number one is that your instructor/coach or teammate has either suggested or asked you to go and watch a point tournament.

Two, you have already been to one or two tournaments and lost all or most of them. Three, you have been to a few fights and have come close to winning the big trophy, but one or two people keep beating you and you can't get past them. If you fall into either of these, this book is probably for you.

In the first scenario we are talking about you being an observer. You are there to learn, but only through observation. Nothing is wrong with that especially if you are new to martial arts and have yet to get your footing. In options two and three you are in the active learning stage of your training. You are like a new cook; you have all of the right ingredients and are trying to get the recipe right for your taste.

If you just stayed as an observer and decided to, just for the heck of it, enter to fight on that day that your friends recommended for you, your odds of winning are at worst 40/60 and at best 50/50.

In the second category, you have only won one, possibly two or maybe none yet. However, you do have some experience under your belt.

On any given day and all things being equal (age, weight, length of time training, some fight experience, you have a 50/50 chance of winning just on sheer luck. In the third and final category it comes down to figuring out why you lost before. This book helps you find out and come up with a solution. If you follow what I say here those odds should move to 70/30.

This book, and your hard work and effort, can help you bridge the gap between being an almost ran to a champ. Of course, nothing in this book can help you if you do not want to put in the hard work and effort that it takes to succeed. Being smart alone will not do it. Having the genetics for it will give you a slight edge. Having technical skills, like genetics, will give you a slight edge. However, hard work and persistence, as it is in everything in this life, is what will get you what you want.

I am not a world-famous coach or, more importantly, fighter, but I have traveled the world. I have been around long enough and experienced enough, that I can evaluate what works and what does not. The insights that I have into fighting will help you get the edge you need to not just win a few fights, but many of them. Think of this book as a set of recipes.

With every good recipe, you will make specific changes here and there to make it yours. Your fights will have a particular flavor to them. I will present you with all the ingredients for a well-rounded meal. After which, you will cook it up and serve your opponents a large plate of whup-ass! The only thing that is required of you is your time and dedication. If you cannot provide that, stop now, and give this book to someone who can.

There will be lots of repetition because science tells us that we must repeat something over and over until our body understands it. I repeat things all the time, mainly because I'm old, but also because repetition helps you learn and internalize what you are studying. After you have learned it, you will not have to force yourself to remember it; it will just come to you.

This book does not require any sort of degree from any sort of school. You should laugh a little because there are moments of humor written here, or at least I hope that there are. This book will not remotely make you an expert in anything. Everything in this book is meant to be applied to not just martial arts but to life, a subject that I have been studying, unsuccessfully, for the last 58 plus years.

At the end of the day, my job is to make you a better fighter, and hopefully, that spills over into other things. Why? Because many of the things that will make you a great fighter will also make you a better person. Remember, you will not compete at fighting all your life. It will only be a small period that will go by faster than you can imagine. However, the life lessons that you learn while training and fighting will last you all your days.

If used correctly, anyone who does point fighting of any type of combat art will use this book to become a better fighter. I don't care if you are a boxer, soldier, marine, mma competitor, or a grandma training for her first martial arts competition; you should do better than you did before or without reading this book. No matter who you are or where you are in your training, this book has something for you.

Not for the last time, I should point out, no pun intended, point tournaments are like any sort of fighting competition and require seriousness of purpose and thought to succeed. This is doubly or triply so in mma (not to be confused with Tripoli in Libya). Your attitude and willingness to work hard will help you move beyond being ordinary.

An unexpected benefit of fighting, even if you do not go to tournaments, is that combat teaches you not to freeze up in fear or shock.

Every business owner, leader or commander of troops, man, or woman, boy or girl, should be put in the ring, on the mat, in the cage, or wherever your combat takes place, and go at it. There is no business school or psychoanalysis that can prepare you better to face challenges, fear, and the unknown like fighting.

Why? Because combat, in the form of a tournament or on the battlefield, helps to wean the weakness of second-guessing out of you. When you get that first smack to the mouth or punch to the eye AND you realize that the pain did not kill you, that's when the fear starts to melt away. There might be a moment of shock that you are still standing, but you stay and don't quit.

Eventually, you will get to the point if you get knocked down, "Hey, that wasn't quite as bad as I thought," and you get up and say, "let's see if they can do that again," with a smile on your face. If you can do this, you have cracked one of the most deeply held primal codes in humans.

It may not happen the first time or even the 100th time, but the fact that you come back to see if you can take it again is proof that you are getting better. You now start to conquer fear. When you do that, you begin to dominate life. Let me take a real-life instance of not letting fear hold you back.

I have a young friend named Adan. Nice kid. He, at one time, was being bullied. Adan is a warm and friendly young man. He also has a beautiful smile and a kind way about him. Kids that he played with started calling him names and taking advantage of him. His mother, a great and longtime friend, asked me what she should do. I recommended martial arts. She, having studied martial arts herself when we were in high school, had thought of this already but needed a second opinion, which I provided.

To make a long story short, he went to a gym that I knew about and started to learn how to fight. One uppercut and a year later, Adan has not been bullied anymore. From what I hear, he is also doing well in his other endeavors, and I think that this can be attributed, in part, to his new confidence. The confidence gained through overcoming fear and plenty of practice.

This book concentrates on training for point competition but has parts that apply to all combat competitions. These point competitions allow for beginner, intermediate and advanced martial artists to compete in a regulated sport. The goal is to see who can "hit" "kick," or "tag" their opponent quickly and hard enough somewhere on the body or head that 2-4 judges and, most importantly, a center referee, can agree would have been a "kill shot" or one that would have caused significant injury if in an actual combat situation. The idea of the "kill shot" is what helped karate and martial arts in general gain popularity in the '60s. It, however, was not until the '70s that point tournaments gained attention in the wider public's eye.

There were several reasons why point tournaments exploded onto the scene back in the 1970s. The first one was that it was a method for showing off how much better a particular school or gyms students were to the others that were popping up all over town. People would see the name of a school and recognize some of the students from a particular school and sign up with them.

Tournaments also gave instructors a way of seeing where their students were at by how well they competed against others outside of their school. It was also a way for them to network. Fighting in the gym and at tournaments is a way for instructors to see how good their students were and how well they were progressing. The next thing was that this was an opportunity to show who was the best between the various styles that were also now on the scene.

Among non-Asian people, the martial arts that most of us are familiar with have been around in the USA and Europe since the late 1800s. Mainly in Europe. In the USA, there were two waves of martial arts interest in the last century.

The first after grandmaster Robert Trias
(shameless plug for my second styles founder) and
other military men and women came back to the
USA after WWII and subsequently the Korean
war.

The original purpose for this sort of training
was so that various martial artists could have their
lesser skilled students compete against one another
and students from other schools without them
injuring one another. Of course, there were lots of
injuries because instructors could not agree on the
rules. There was also an issue of safety. When I
started in the late 1970s, few people wore any sort
of safety equipment.

There was, from the beginning, a wide range
of opinions on how hard a punch or kick should
be. After all, this was a martial art that manifested

itself in a combat sport. There were some that argued that what they did could never be a sport because its techniques were too vicious and devastating. That argument still exists even to this day.

What is important is that, even though it changes constantly, we agree that we do not want our students to be maimed or hurt unnecessarily. What happens to them is part of the learning process. This learning process will continue from the first day that they walk through our doors to the very last day that they are able to train. Combat sports will always have an element of danger to them. There is no way around this. What the instructor and coach must do is help to alleviate as much of the causes of pain

Of course, the question that I'm sure you are most wanting to be answered is, "how do I kick someone's butt and win a trophy or medal?" The answer is simple, train hard, long, and more often than your opponents do. To win a fight of any sort, competitive or life and death, it always helps if you are bigger, stronger, faster, flexible, and smarter than your opponent.

To answer the question that gave us the title of this section: Why buy this book? I will provide you with the details and processes that you need to make sure that you become an elite-level fighter. All the major things that you need to be a success are here. You just need to do the actual work of getting to the gym consistently and putting in the work. You will get better, and you will become an elite fighter. That is why you should buy this book.

Chapter 1: What Are Tournaments for and Who Goes to Them

This book is not about me, but I think I represent the typical person that went to tournaments back in the day (the 1970's and early 80's) and continues to do so now. Please pardon me for the autobiographical parts, but I use them as a tool to make various points. Hopefully, you will see the relevance by the end of the book. Let's start by answering the question, "what are tournaments for"?

Tournaments are places to learn how to use the fighting techniques you have learned in school or the gym. Tournaments are a fun way to widen your network of friends but, more importantly, potential sparring partners. Rudimentary fighting takes place, but it should not be considered "real world" fighting. I will say it now and probably a hundred more times before the last word is read here, tournament fighting is a game of tag done at high speed.

They are usually recommended by instructors for two reasons. First, they want you to compete against people who are not from your school. The logic is, if you practice with the same people all the time, you learn to recognize their moves, and you know how to counter them. As the saying goes, you don't want to fish in the same part of the pond all the time. Fighting is the same way; you can't grow and become better if you are fighting the same people day in and day out. The person who attacks you on the street or battlefield is probably not working out with you daily.

At a tournament, everyone is new and has different ways of fighting, or at least they do against you. It allows you to use other techniques and learn if what you have trained on is practical to a certain degree. I absolutely agree that I became a better fighter by fighting people who were not in my style or dojo. I believe this to be true pretty much for everyone, then and now. This, in fact, is a testable theory.

Take any student or athlete who has been working out for a year to two years. To test this, you need a class of at least 30 students who started within at least 2 to 3 months of each other. Randomly take six students to compete at an open tournament. Isolate them from the rest of their class or team for three months. Send them to at least six open matches on consecutive weekends in a row.

I will promise you that they will come back better than they did prior to going to the tournament. In fact, I will wager that they are now at least equal or slightly better in fighting, not kata or technical skills than they were before they went. Their reaction time and ring knowledge will now be better. At least it will be in the short term. Why? Because they have been introduced to a broader world of fighters and, thus, a wider world of possibilities.

The second reason to go to a tournament, which happens in every country and almost all disciplines, is that schools want to show everyone how good they are. This is one of the reasons why most tournaments are open and public. The Blue Lotus Praying Mantis Kung Fu school wants to show the public and other martial arts schools that they are more demanding than master Kang's

Taekwondo Tigers. Both schools want to outshine the Rising Sun Karate Academy. In large cities, this is a huge factor because winning a tournament is a significant mode of advertisement for them.

There is also a third reason. Economics. A well-run and well-attended tournament can bring in a lot of revenue. I know of several dojo's that make the bulk of their money not from their school and students but from the tournaments that they hold. Far fewer schools do this now, but it is still a big reason why some organizations sponsor contests.

There is a very popular school in California that teaches several disciplines. It's not a big gym, but it makes 70% of its annual revenue from the tournaments that it holds. Less than 20% of its annual revenue comes from monthly dues.

I grew up in the 1970s and, kind of like it is now, how you have mma gyms everywhere and Jiu-Jitsu is the only thing that anyone wants to study, kung fu was it. Why, because of Bruce Lee. The seminal moment is that opening scene from "Enter the Dragon." If you want to see where mma really comes from, this is the scene for you. Unfortunately for me, I didn't see this movie for years afterward because my mother thought this sort of thing was too violent for her baby. This was, of course, part of my problem.

I was a little kid and was picked on a lot. I was such a weakling that the boys close to me in age shunned me. I was relegated to playing with the girls my age. My uncle Billie felt so sorry for me that he taught me martial arts. I point this out because I was so pathetic and needed protection so bad that he took the time to teach me.

He didn't even teach his kids, who were admittedly younger than I was. On a side note, my uncle's sons, Eric and Kasey, were considerably younger than I was and still tougher than I ever was. It wasn't until I made it to high school that I learned how to defend myself better.

I attended Nicholas Senn High School, which is located on the north side of Chicago. For my high school, as far as I know, we were the first large group of people of color. We were from the south and west sides.

This was the era of bussing and integration, which meant that there were parents and students who were not fond of my friends and me being students there. However, there was a very vocal group that wanted to let me and my friends absolutely understand that we were not welcomed.

They were called the TJO's. I want to go into what that stood for, but I don't see how it was complementary to them.

To shorten this story some, people who ultimately became my friends banded together to walk from the train station to the school and back to the train so as not to get beat up. To be honest, I think that they got together to protect me. Of those that were male and became friends with me, all knew some form of martial art. Despite how this sounds, we were not a gang. We did, however, give ourselves a gang-like nickname.

Don't laugh, and please remember that this was in the middle part of the seventies, and Kung Fu movies were at the height of their popularity. We were the **Kung Fu Duks**! Yes, the Kung Fu Duks. I was not part of the naming of our group.

At the time, I was more of a follower. But we were an aspirational organization.

Leonard Cosby knew Shaolin Kung Fu; the Shackleford brothers did taekwondo, Carlos Davis practiced Shotokan karate, I believe. Devon did Jiu-jitsu and judo, Adam Kemp some form of karate, Thurman Turner, Tony, and Michael "Red Cloud" Moore weren't martial artists but were tough. These brothers were real street fighters, but in the ancient sense. Thurman was extra cool because he loved to smack guys with a rolled-up copy of his Chicago Sun-Times. Once I saw him smack a guy so hard that he gave Thurman his wallet. Thurman then went and spent that money on his future wife, Sherry. True story.

This was my second phase of real martial arts. After a while, people started to think that I, through osmosis, I guess, knew martial arts. I categorically did not, at least not yet, but because of my fellow Kung Fu Duks, people thought that I did. This became very evident when I got invited to fight someone in public and in front of other people who everyone knew could fight.

My high school was huge and had tiny crevices where you could get together either totally out of sight or at least long enough where you didn't have to worry about teachers or other unwanted eyes bothering you. Our place was behind the gym behind some high bushes.

As I mentioned, in my freshmen year, there was a huge influx of people of color. Not just those of African American descent (there were also others of African descent that I was just realizing that existed such as Jamaicans, Haitians,

Dominicans, Puerto Ricans, Brazilians and other Afro/LatinX folks who I knew nothing about until I got here), but south and south east Asian lineage. In particular, very large groups of Chinese, Korean, Indian, Cambodian, and Vietnamese ancestry. I became friends with Richard Ng (Chinese American) and Brian Cho (Korean American). Both were practitioners of martial arts that came from the countries that their parents immigrated from.

One day, while waiting for my buddies to get out of class so that I wouldn't have to go home alone, I was caught by Richard practicing a spinning back kick that one of the Shackleford brothers had shown me how to do. I wasn't that good at it, but I loved it and practiced it as often as I could.

Richard told Brian about it. When I saw both at lunch the next day, Brian said that he wanted to see my kick and that I might want to come and work out with them the very next day. I said okay.

It was the spring of 1976. I and about 15 young Asian guys were ready to work out. They all knew some type of fighting style. Among the Chinese guys, the most practiced style was Hung Gar (this is a southern Chinese style sometimes called Hung Ga). This is what is sometimes known as an animal style.

The Korean boys all did traditional Taekwondo (they called it something else, I want to say shin shun do, but I am positive that I am mistaken) that they learned from of all places the "Peace School." All of them wanted to see what this Black kid could do.

I met them in the gym where a couple of the Chinese kids were practicing ping pong (a very popular pastime in the "70s). As soon as I got there, we all walked to the back of the gym, almost directly behind the gym teacher's office. A few people that walked out started warming up as soon as we got behind the bushes. About 15 minutes later, a couple of guys got together and started to fight.

Although I didn't know it at the time, this was a "fight club." These sorts of things were very popular. They were like miniature tournaments that happened periodically. It was very impressive, but of course, I didn't know what the hick I was looking at back then. After the 3rd set of guys had played around, Richard told me that it was my turn.

I got smacked around quite a bit. Then just as this Korean kid was about to attack me, that was when I did my spin back kick. I knocked the air out of him. What I didn't know was that he was sick and was taking it easy on me. I found this out almost a year later. Luckily no one else knew this except Brian. We became friends. Brian, in fact, invited me to my first tournament.

Our sophomore year in high school, my friend Brian received his brown belt and was going to compete in his very first open tournament. He asked me if I wanted to see him fight. I said yes. I should point out that I had seen him spar at school, but never against anyone who wasn't in taekwondo.

I wasn't that impressed by his fighting; he wasn't as confident as he normally was. Part of that was because he wasn't sure of the rules at this open tournament. Even though I wasn't that impressed with him on this particular day, I was at the array of styles at the tournament. It was at this tournament that I met Mr. Ken Knudson, who owned something called a dojo in Chicago and the suburbs. He gave me a business card, and I gave that to my dad.

This sort of introduction to martial arts, as I alluded to earlier, was not unusual. Martial arts schools of all types had posters for tournaments on their front doors and the windows of their schools. Their students, who predominantly went to public schools, talked about them even if they were not going to them. The tournaments were social events, and everyone wanted to go to them.

About two weeks after I gave my dad the business card, he asked me to meet him at his office after I got out of school. This wasn't that unusual. I often stopped by to see him on my way home. However, when he specifically asked me to do it, it usually meant that something cool was happening or that I was getting some money. Both were okay with me.

My last class let out at 3:30. I hung out with a few of my friends and then headed downtown. When I got to my father's office, he was just talking to someone that worked for him. My dad worked at Chicago's city hall, and I loved coming to see him there. As usual, when I walked into his office, I headed to my favourite place, his luxurious couch. He was telling someone a joke while at the same time giving them instructions as to how to do something. My dad had a black belt in comedy.

We talked for a few minutes before he told me that he wanted me to get a job and that I needed to become a more responsible person, and a job would facilitate that. He added that I was getting older and needed to start acting like a man more. To be both a better man and a better person, he was going to need some help. To that end, he had talked to his brother-in-law and my uncle, Mr. Elzie "Billy" Winters.

My uncle Billie was a short and often serious guy. Now you would call him focused. He also had a stutter. Normally, this combination of things would prevent him from being in the inner circle of people that my father would hang out with.

When you are talking about the exact opposite of someone, here is where you had it.

My dad was Mr. Cool. In fact, people often called him *Joe Cool.* Funny, well-dressed, intelligent, tall, and cool. Cool was not what my uncle Billy had, but something that he did have that my dad thought was remarkable was that he had studied karate in Japan, and to my dad, that was super cool or, as my dad would call it, "James Bond" cool! So, when my dad wanted to know if he should sign me up with this Ken Knudsen guy, he went straight to Uncle Billy.

My uncle told him that he had already started training me but only part-time. He advised my father that he would continue training me but agreed that it would be better if I went someplace that would be more hands-on and consistent than what he had been doing with me. He agreed to look around for a place for me to train. He told my dad that he would check out a few spots and get back with him if he thought any of them were worth it.

In no time at all, he came back with a list of places for him to sign me up. One place was the YMCA, not that far from where I lived. There was also a place near the Sears office over near Taylor Avenue. Another place was on Belmont, just off the train. Last, but not least was Mr. Knudson's place right near my father's office. Years later, I found out that he had gone to all three places but liked the Y the best. My dad decided on Mr. Knudson's "Olympic Karate Studios" because it was within walking distance of his office, and he could check up on me.

My instructor was Mr. Mike Rivas. Talk about talking fast and fast hands! Sensei Mike was the man! He was a student and in law school at DePaul University. Olympic Karate Studios was a great place to learn martial arts, not just Karate. In fact, this is probably the place that I was first introduced to the idea of mixed martial arts, although in a non-formal way.

Everyone came to our school. Black, white, Hispanic, Asian, male, female, straight, and gay. If you wanted to throw down, you came here or stopped off here to get there. Everyone, when I signed up, was a purple belt and up.

To use an old metaphor for the second time, these folks "threw down." You came here to fight. I, on the other hand, only came to learn self-defence.

The great thing about Olympic Karate Studios is that it was still at a time where we were traditional in our training, but we were also adding other items. If you were a student here, you had to bring it.

If I remember correctly, there were, we had a minimum of two mandatory classes a week, and yes, you learned kata. One of those days required grappling and throwing training. Two days for the brown belts and up was weapons training. Three days were for self-defense, and then you had everything else.

We were not required, but nudged strongly, to go to tournaments and fight and or do kata's (forms) and/or weapons forms. Most people would do two events because it cost the same no matter what. Some of the tournaments even had black belt full-contact fighting. These were the beginning of point fighting's hay days.

Tournaments were held everywhere. Schools, churches, synagogues, mosques, and even theatres would have tournaments. Usually, they would start early in the morning, around 8 or 9, for sign-in, and forms would be first up.

Start with the youngsters, then teens and adults and seniors last. Weapons in the same order and finally sparring. Black belt fighting was at the very end of the tournament. That is pretty much what it has remained since.

Like a lot of old people, I'm going to say that fighting was harder back in our day. In this case, it is true. Back then, you could kick to the groin as a yellow belt. You can't do that even at the black belt level at some places now.

We would practice what was called a slip kick (this was a very low roundhouse kick shot from the lead leg and aimed below the navel and somewhere above the knees.) In the late 70's we did have safety equipment, but it was not mandatory to wear.

On your fist, you may have seen someone who wore this thin gauze around their knuckles, but that was it. Nothing on the feet, and occasionally, I saw someone with a safety cup on. Point tournaments were not a "tag" event yet. As a green belt, I saw a kid at a big tournament (bigger tournaments were safer tournaments) get a rib cracked. Everyone was tough.

The few women who fought were amazing. I was excited about fighting and wanted to share that excitement with everyone. One person I shared it with was my girlfriend, Barbara.

Barbara was a musician and believed that you must share your art with others. She thought that martial arts were like fine arts. To get better at them, you had to spend a lot of time practicing.

She told me once that when you attained a certain level of skill, it was time to explore different segments of your art. She was correct about this. I was getting better and was one of the better students at my dojo, or at least I thought that I was. It was time for me to try something else.

At this point, I had already started to get interested in other arts. My buddies at my high school who were "Kung Fu Duks" (I'll explain this later) all were practitioners of various styles. One friend, who was not a "Kung Fu Duk," was a guy named Perry Archie.

My good friend Perry (Now Dr. and Pastor, Perry Archie – so proud of this man), was a big Bruce Lee fan and a Kung Fu practitioner, advised me to come to the Boys and Girls club and work out with him. He said that they were thinking about having a kickboxing class and wanted to know if I would be interested.

The following Saturday, I picked up Barbara from a concert that she had played at and went to see my buddy, Perry. We worked out a little, and I met the kickboxing coach. He was very charismatic. The following Tuesday after that, I started kickboxing with Sensei/coach Ken Stephens. The location was the Boys and Girls Club just north of Lawrence Avenue on Sheridan

Road. At that time, it was not the nicest neighbourhood.

I loved the class because I knew some of the guys that were in it, and they made it fun for me. The only problem was that it was hard. Hard and painful. Coach Ken kicked our butts in this class! There were no belts. Our coach/sensei was, as they say now, a beast. He was a former Green Beret who believed you should leave your opponent dead, incapacitated, or some third option that combined the two.

Because of his military training, he was adamant about us using techniques that were efficient. He wanted us to be well-rounded fighters. In fact, he told me to join the wrestling team so that I could have a ground game. I didn't understand that back then, but now I do.

Most of my friends didn't understand it either and didn't do it. We went full throttle. We were fit, young, rock hard, and could plow through anyone. Or so we thought. In my senior year in high school, our coach took us to our first standard tournament.

We had to go to a standard tournament because there were no places that had full contact outside of Western boxing, where we were sanctioned to fight. Some of us had done some underground fighting, which was hugely popular, but there just wasn't enough of it.

For some reason, coach Ken did not approve of this at all, so to give us an outlet, he said we would go to an open-style tournament to fight. He did warn us that the people that we would meet, will not fight like us, so the rules would be different from what we were used to or practiced.

When I look back on time and how we were trained and just what was going on, I can see how and why we didn't do well. I can't think of the name of the tournament, but I do remember seeing some guys from Olympic Karate Studio's there. I didn't see Sensei Mike, but I did see some of the other black belts from the school and some of the others that my buddy had competed against.

I honestly don't remember how we did as individuals, but I do remember how things went for us. It was a disaster for us. We kept getting dinged for excessive force and were disqualified. Everyone but the three of us who had started in other more traditional schools was disqualified.

Everyone that had "started" with Sensei/coach Ken lost. I have to say that the judges were right because our guys hit hard. Even when they started to grasp what light contact was, the power of our striking made our opponents want to quit.

Now I can see why that happened, but only because of the years that have come and gone. I'm happy with what we accomplished and that it happened, but sad that it can't be repeated. I consider myself lucky to have had training in point fighting and full contact kickboxing during this time. It helped to make me a better fighter. What we did was one of the precursors to modern MMA.

All of this brings us to the point of this chapter. Everyone who likes fisticuffs goes to tournaments of one type and venue. If you are interested in athletics in its rawest form, you are a fan probably without even knowing it. Combat sports of all and any type are about competition, and point competition is just one variant of that.

I should make you aware, as if you were not already, that point competition is just that it is a competition. In the martial arts, overall, it is special because it is a training exercise and a guide for instructors. It is not the purpose of martial arts!

Since it is a form of combat competition, it is a great training ground for those that think that they may want to try something more aggressive one day. I am obligated to point out that tournaments and combat competitions of all types are forms of entertainment.

The Colosseum's of ancient Rome and Greece were staged for fighters just as Broadway was and is a stage for actors in theatre. Both are places for the masses to be entertained. Fighting is, in certain instances and venues, a form of entertainment. Who goes to tournaments? People who want to be entertained and those learning the craft of it.

Chapter 2: Who Should Study Martial Arts

I personally think that everyone should take some form of martial arts. It could be Taekwondo, Karate, Judo, Jiu Jitsu, Muay Thai or Kung Fu. It could also be western-style boxing or wrestling, but whatever you decide on taking, it should be something that you enjoy and that challenges you mentally and physically.

If you are a parent, there are two things you should know. First, let your kids be part of the decision-making process in picking a school to train at. They are going to work at it a lot better and stay in it longer, if you let them be part of picking a gym to train in. If they like it, they will practice harder and stay with it longer, but more importantly, if you let them be part of the decision process, it will save you some money. As a parent, I'm all about saving money!

Number two join the class with your child. A family that trains together works better together. Training together encourages teamwork, fosters family cohesion, and is simply more fun. My experience as a teacher has shown me that when a family works out together that their family bonds become tighter and last a lifetime.

A good friend of mine asked me, not that long ago, why should my daughter take martial arts? Shouldn't I only let my sons do it? The first thing that I told him was that he was being sexist. Then I asked him why he wanted his sons to learn how to fight? His answer was that he just wanted to make sure that if they had to, that they could kick some butt.

My response to that was, "well, why wouldn't you want that for your daughter? "Girls can kick butt too!" Of course, there are other reasons and benefits to learning martial arts besides being able to kick butt. Let's talk about some of them now.

There are a host of benefits that a person, especially a child, gets from studying martial arts. To be honest with you, gender and sex rarely play any part in it. This is especially true when they are at the pee wee age (5 -7) and (8 – 12). If I am not mistaken, the strength differences don't become apparent or start until around 13 or 14 years old.

For kids, it's not the gender that plays a part in if they are good or how well or fast that they learn fighting skills. It, as it is as an adult, comes down to drive, motivation, and support. No matter what the gender of that child is.

The best reasons are discipline, health, and self-confidence. Of these reasons, at the top is discipline. This is such an important topic; I have dedicated a whole chapter to it.

When I taught, the greatest compliment that I received from a parent was that their child's grades started to improve. Next up would be that their child is more well-behaved and disciplined. There is nothing better than hearing that your student is, no matter the age, has become a better person!

This commonly, across the board and spectrum of behavior and personality types, happens most significantly with kids who have had disciplinary issues. As a side effect, the more control that they have over themselves, the better the grades sometimes get.

Another impact from training in the martial arts that I saw from my students and others training in martial arts is that they demonstrated more confidence. Martial arts training and combat training in general provides those that study and train hard with confidence because they can achieve certain goals and accomplishments.

I often talk about why martial arts are good for kids, but they are also great for seniors. Electronic gaming is not active enough, nor does it utilize enough muscles or muscle groups to cause a person of any size or shape to sweat or get tired. Due to this lack of energetic play, electronic games fail miserably in the parent's goal of tiring their kids out enough so that they go to bed and pass out from exhaustion, not to reawaken until at least the parent's 2nd coffee of the morning and preferably after some sort of breakfast.

As I mentioned at the very beginning of this section, the number one reason why most people bring their kids to me and other martial artists is to learn discipline. Just the act of learning discipline, as it has historically been taught and thought of in America, Europe, and other places in the world, calls for you also to learn some other things that are desirable in life.

Unfortunately, parents and others really do not understand how it works or what we do to impart it. The things that our students and disciples gain are sometimes intrinsic at the beginning and further on but have such an impact, for the better, that their value is incalculable.

Some of those things are learning to set goals, understanding honor, sticking to it ness, respect, conflict resolution, and even humor. The most significant and most important part of discipline and something that the military has done throughout history provides its warriors with strict regimentation in the form of strict guidelines of behavior in the school, training area, or gym. A fighter's life has a high degree of regimentation.

What is regimentation? It's all about having the action done in a very structured fashion. Performing small steps towards the completion of something or the practice of something over and over is part of a goal and with a purpose. Cleaning your uniform and folding it a particular way each and every time is part of the regimentation that you go through. It is a crucial aspect of learning discipline.

Chapter 3: The Purpose and Benefits of Martial Arts

Martial means war. A synonym would be military. Martial arts are the arts of war and the ways of the military when it comes to self-defense. In modern times (anything after 1945 CE), it means all combat arts or fighting of any type between two or more (but less than four people) and without weapons, unless those weapons are non-ballistic, i.e., guns, rifles, canons, mines of any type or form. A catch-all phrase would be a hand-to-hand battle. This self-defense aspect is at the core of martial arts and even the competitive versions of those arts.

In all the world, China has the most famous group of martial arts practitioners, and they are the

Shaolin monks. These monks, at one time, led very ascetic lives and found virtue in not being attached to material things or goals. They also denied themselves many urges of the flesh.

Because they meditated for long periods of time, sometimes hours on end, they exhibited the outcome of living such sedentary lives. They became weak, gaunt, and listless. Stories handed down to us through the centuries tell us that this changed when Bodhidharma arrived at the Shan monastery in Henan Provence.

When Bodhidharma arrived, things started to change. Before he came, the monks had become easy pickings for brigands and thieves that would pounce upon the monks when they strayed too far from the refuge of the monastery. Due to their lack of physical strength or any physical skill whatsoever, the monks could mount no defense for their personal wellbeing or of the small tokens that they would receive for alms (alms are donations of food or money that they would receive for followers and well-wishers). Bodhidharma changed all of this.

All the martial arts that are outside of their countries of origin came to the shores of the west, mainly the Americas and Europe, via troops or merchant marines that had been stationed in the South east of Asia at one time or another. They did not come here as a gift or through cultural exchanges, although this did happen in the late '50s, '60s, and even '70s.

Up until the late 1800s, the most popular martial art in the world was judo. In 1918 the Budokwai was founded in London, England. It was founded by Gunji Koizumi, who taught judo, Jiu-Jitsu, and Kendo. In the late '50s and early 60's karate, Tae Kwon Do and Aikido were added to the roster.

Most of the students were military (Navy and Marines), from military families, police (former military), or from the families of diplomats. This makes sense because these were the people who would have first contact with the outside world. This group pattern would be the same in all European countries. Eventually, these same groups would sponsor, or send for their teachers or their representatives, to come to their respective countries and start to teach others.

This process would repeat itself after every new excursion to Southeast Asia and after every military conflict. In the USA and Canada, it happened with the Korean conflict in the 1950s. Soldiers, sailors, marines, and airmen would come in contact with Tae Kwon Do, Karate, Judo, and Jiu-Jitsu on the post and in the communities that they frequented.

Even in the earlier iterations of contact, it was almost the same and with the exact same martial arts. With the later generations, it was different. In particular, immediately at the waning days of Vietnam and at the end, there was a new way of martial evangelization. At this point, there were two distinct waves.

First, the Kung Fu movie craze of the '70s and two decades later with the advent of MMA and the start of the UFC. Both time periods are of extreme historical significance and play a major role in how mma, Jiu-Jitsu, and the combat arts started a new level of ascendancy in the world's cultural awareness.

In this new martial arts fervor, competition of the full contact type was now supreme. Full contact fighting, in the form of mixed martial arts as espoused by the UFC, was not just a fighting style but a new way of being in shape and achieving "ultimate" fitness. This new fitness paradigm is promoted not only by the organizations that the fighters hold allegiance to but is key to their identities as athletes.

We will talk about the benefits of martial arts and its practice in one way or another throughout this book. For now, we are going to talk about the absolute best and what I consider to be, again in my eyes, the top ones. I'm sure that this will apply to both sides of the corn, traditionalist and modern. First, let's delineate the main differences between the two.

The traditionalist likes, no loves, to tell us how the masters of old persevered over their foes. I understand this but would suggest, as must historians do, history is written by the victors. There will be, by the very nature of things, a certain tint to what is only apocryphal information. This does not make less true, but a grain of salt should be brought to the table.

We do know that specific exercises and drills were practiced with the goal of giving the martial artist certain skill sets. To that end, the first book that I am aware of and one that (before this book) provided the most detailed and was the most comprehensive of its type was *"Karate; The Art of*

Empty-Handed Fighting" by Hidetaka Nishiyama and Richard C. Brown.

As I have probably mentioned before, and I promise you I will mention it again, this book was given to me by my first instructor, my uncle Elzie "Billy" Winters. He was an Airman in the United States Air Force in Japan in the 1960s. He reached the level of brown belt in Jiu-jitsu and Shotokan karate.

According to him, it was also a requirement to study judo, which was taught by the instructor that taught him Jiu-jitsu. At the time, there were only two belts, white and black, just before he started. During his second tour, the brown belt was introduced. It was a very new thin belt but was given to him before he left Okinawa in 1972.

His experience is not uncommon at all. I mentioned this a few paragraphs earlier. In fact, I would venture to say that it was the most common way for the seed of martial arts to be planted. As it was in earlier waves of martial arts flowering, military people like my uncle were stationed in South East Asia.

While there, they were able to meet specific cultural and social habits of the indigenous people. In Japan, Karate, during the '50s and '60s, was still reasonably new. It technically had only been practiced for 30 or so years in Japan. About the same length of time that Brazilian Jiu-Jitsu has been practiced in the United States right now

My uncle and thousands of other Airmen, Soldiers, Marines, and Sailors learned what they could either on the base or near it. When their tour of duty was up, they brought what they had learned here. Some learned very well and had advanced quickly while in Asia. Others came back with just minimal training and started to teach what they knew.

They knew just enough to show someone who was knowledgeable that they really did know something, but they were not good or experienced enough to teach the art in a correct or professional manner. This, in part, accounts for the lack of consistency in quality among schools of the same style and lineage.

While this has caused some problems in the quality of education and historical cohesion, the martial arts culture has survived and thrives today. The reason for this, I believe, is that you have a large enough "free market," and the consumer (students, coaches, teachers, and parents) have lots of options. Because there is such a large marketplace, there is lots of competition. The best comes out of this milieu. Students of all types benefit, and so does society. (By the way, yes, I am a capitalist pig!)

Chapter 4 – Learning Discipline and Self Improvement

This chapter is one of the most important chapters in this book. If used right, it will be the chapter that will put you on the road to being a champion. Not just in fighting, but in life. It is the secret sauce to becoming enlightened. Self-control and discipline are part of the keys towards happiness, absolute freedom, and learning the meaning of life.

"*True freedom is impossible without a mind made free by discipline.*"

- Mortimer J. Adler

One of the things that separate martial arts training, and the activity of combat sports is the idea of explicitly being taught self-control and discipline with the goal of achieving improvement of self. In fact, many traditional martial artists believe that it is not about being a better fighter but being a better human. Discipline, or the idea of discipline, causes many people great anxiety.

For our purposes, and I mean this for all martial arts and combat sports, discipline is a tool and a process used by various stakeholders. If you are the coach or instructor, it is a tool utilized to develop and incentivize your student. If you are the athlete/student, it is a process by which you gain confidence and grow physically and mentally. Without it, you fail.

When I was a much younger person, I joined the Army. I consider myself as having been a good soldier. I was not that at the beginning. I was just okay at basic training, which is where you learn the basics of being a soldier. I did well at my AIT (advanced individual training) phase. I didn't become a good soldier until my first day at my first duty station in Mannheim, Germany.

I was picked up in an open jeep, no top or sides in the middle of winter, from Rhein-Main Air Force base in Frankfort, Germany. My escort was a Private McNutt, who had just prior to picking me up, had been a Sargent/E5. He was one of the nicest guys that I met in my entire time in the military. He was also the first person to give me some great advice.

Private (henceforth pvt) drove me in the cold of a German winter and talked nonstop for the 38 or so miles from Frankfort to Mannheim. He told me who my duty station commander would be, along with the names of the officers under his command. He told me what NCO's (noncommissioned officers) to go to for help, but the real thing that he said that had lasted me through the years is to always display "good" discipline.

I remember asking him what this meant. He said that discipline means to bring to a state of order and obedience by training and control. A month later, I found out that he had stolen that line from an ex-Marine. Either way, it was and is good advice for soldiers and people in general who want their lives and what they do to be more organized and successful.

You, according to many traditional Chinese, Korean, and Japanese teachers, should become better through the study of martial arts, physically, emotionally, socially, and spiritually when compared to your average person. Becoming a good fighter is just a bonus of being a good person. In this chapter, I will talk about a few techniques you can use to start on the path to achieving a higher degree of discipline. By learning discipline, you can become a truly elite fighter.

"The ultimate aim of Karate-do is to build character, conquer human misery and find spiritual freedom" - Attributed to Miyagi Chojun, founder of Goju-Ryu

A person who I greatly admire is Admiral William H. McRaven. He was a member of the Navy's SEAL Team 4 and 6 and commanded SEAL Team 3. He served in Desert Storm and Operation Desert Shield. He has been both a warrior in the thick of battle and a consultant to business and political leaders in his life.

One of the things that he recommends when asked about how to become more disciplined and focused is to wake up, and before you do anything else, is to make up your bed. I know it sounds like a little thing, but when you think about it, it is not.

You could so easily just roll out of bed and start other things such as showering, eating, and going about your day. With it, you have created and set a goal, then you have accomplished it. Your day starts with a small success!

Starting things off by doing a small task helps you get your day organized. It is a foundation for the rest of your day. It is a little thing, but little things add up to greater things. You start your day off with a sense of accomplishment. You have achieved something good, and that begins your day with a

This next technique has two parts to it. The first one is to write down your to-do list for the day. It should have a spot for you to check off on if you have or have not accomplished it. Do not create it with the aid of a computer. In fact, do not put it on any device at all. Use pen and paper.

Afterward, post it somewhere that you must pass or look at. I believe that when you take the time to write it, you are making it real. This is your list of things that you must accomplish for the day. You must look at it before you end your day, and it will help guide you for the next day's list.

This little thing gives your day direction. You have a purpose now for how you move throughout the day. You have a path to accomplishing things in an organized way. I believe that it was *Steven Covey* who wrote a book about the seven habits of successful people. One of the things that he recommended was to write out what you were to do for the day, every day. Included in that things to do was to have fun and relax.

I should point out, although I shouldn't have to do this, that it is important that you have fun and love in your life. It is important that you have joy and love with the people who you like to have fun with and who you love.

Remember when you go to that job or when you compete, you are doing these things not just for you, but for those who are a part of you. When you put must-do things on your to-do list, the thing that you must do is have time for them to share your life's journey.

One of the first things that I learned about elite people (not just point fighters but businesspeople, entertainers, scientists, and successful people of all stripes) is that they are able to visualize and see themselves being successful at whatever it is that they set out to do. Visualization, seeing how you are going to become successful, and seeing AND believing that you are successful, are key elements in becoming an elite champion.

Pick a point during the day when you have a moment and visualize yourself becoming a successful fighter. You have to see yourself as achieving whatever your goal is. Envision yourself raising that trophy up in the air and your team and friends surrounding you and congratulating you on what you have accomplished. If you can't picture it, neither can anyone else. Visualization is very important in how you will become a success, not just as an elite fighter but as a businessperson and a member of human society.

"The ultimate aim of Karate lies not in victory or defeat, but in the perfection of the character of its participants." - Gichin Funakoshi, father of Shotokan Karate

Gichin Funakoshi believed that the goal of Karate was not to teach a person how to fight but to make them a better person. He, and his followers, taught that when you train the body through rigorous physical training that you tap into something that is beyond the obvious and not intuitive. Similar to what many ancient ascetics thought, Buddha, included that through hard, focused work, that one can raise their consciousness. Ultimately one can become more enlightened.

I had the honor of visiting Japan when I was a younger man. As a martial artist, I had hoped that while I was there that I would have the opportunity to work out at a famous dojo, but that did not happen. However, something better happened. I met a student of master Funakoshi! His name was Hiroshi Tanada. I was introduced to him through one of the military staff members that I was working with while I was there.

We talked for about two hours, and then he invited me to have dinner with several of his students. I did not and still do not speak Japanese. His students did so but only slightly. So, the entire evening he had to translate. While enjoying the meal and their company, I, of course, had to talk about fighting and training. I found it amazing that they all were very modern in how they trained.

They utilized weights, calisthenics, cross-training in other styles of fighting, and training that I never thought that they would have even considered that they would have thought of. Of course, this just shows that I was being an arrogant American. I just assumed that we were the only ones that thought that using "non-traditional" ways of training was legitimate.

This was the first time that I had heard directly that there were schools in Japan that taught Jiu-Jitsu, Judo, boxing, and Karate all in one place. I have to say; it was not considered MMA. Not all students are trained this way. It was only for those that were black belts. I never knew why that was the case.

Although this was unusual, it wasn't out of the realm to me. What was unusual was that each of them told me that calligraphy (traditional writing in Kanji, the official alphabet of the Japanese language) was a part of their students' training.

I had heard of this but only thought that this was something that the ancient Samurai had done. I was surprised. It was not until years later that I found out that certain European military officer training (notably the French, German and British) had made it a requirement that cadets write letters. Why, because it required them to think. To plan out what they would say and how they would say it.

"The first and best victory is to conquer self." - Plato

As a technique for learning discipline, this is a great tool. Make this part of your training just as you would make sure that you run, do jumping jacks, and spar; you should make sure that you write three letters a week to someone. All you need is a paper, pen, an envelope, and a stamp. Emails do not count. Using your computer does not matter because it is too easy.

Think about an older relative, a friend who lives out of state that you have been planning to visit but just have not had the time to see. A letter would be great. It shows caring, attention and thoughtfulness. Writing a letter, as it is with making up your bed, is a little thing, but it builds into something greater.

"Courtesy, Integrity, Perseverance, Self-control and Indomitable spirit. "- The Tenets of Tae Kwon Do

This next technique is very hard for the modern person, but I believe is key to having a stress-free life. This exercise will help you focus, become well-rested and thoughtful. It will also help you wind down and become relaxed. It is a habit that you should perform every day. An hour before you go to bed, turn off all your electronic devices and read a book. It can be a novel, a work of non-fiction, Bible, Torah, or Quran, but whatever it is, it must interest you.

Like the other exercises, you must actively plan, schedule, and follow through on it for it to work. Each of these actions leads to something greater. Each part is an investment towards a better you. This exercise prepares you for bed by relaxing you because it takes your mind away from everything that you did at training and other parts of the day.

When your mind is calm and at ease, the body follows. This allows for a deeper and more restful sleep. This, in turn, lets you wake up 8 hours later, calm and relaxed and ready to take on the world!

Many people fear discipline. They believe that it traps them in a vice. With discipline, some believe that their ability to express themselves is hindered and stifled. I say nay to this. Having self-control and being able to walk freely in public with few or any antagonism is a benefit of learning self-discipline.

Self-control allows you to work within certain societal dictated structures and teaches you to be more open-minded. It provides you with a sense of self-worth and confidence. With self-discipline, you are self-assured. You are the master of your fate and the captain of your soul. Without

it, you are wild and cast about the seas of failure.

Chapter 5: Let Us Start at The Beginning – Your First Steps

Start by doing 1 push-up.
Start by drinking 1 cup of water.
Start by paying toward 1 debt.
Start by reading 1 page.
Start by deleting 1 old contract.
Start by walking 1 lap.
Start by attending 1 event.
Start by writing 1 paragraph.
Start today. Repeat tomorrow.
-   *Unknown*

There will be a "first time" for everything that you do. Learning how to do anything has a first time and your first steps. For a champion, there is the first time that you decided that this is what you wanted for yourself.

I_____ (fill in your name) want to be the state champ in Shotokan or Kung Fu. You probably remember the exact moment when you said that out loud so that you could hear yourself say it. You also probably remember the first person you told that to if you are even remotely serious about achieving this goal.

Of course, having said it means jack squat if you did not act on saying it. If you did act on it, you did so by actively looking for a school. This was another first step. Your next first step would have been to walk through the door of your newly found gym and speak to either the instructor or coach there. At that time, you will explain why you are there and what your goal is. At this point, most people don't say that they want to be an elite fighter or world champion. Usually, they tell the world and everyone, at first something way different but less embarrassing.

Your next first step is your first workout. You are testing the waters and checking out the environment. If you can survive that first class, you can survive the rest. You go to a few classes and decide that you can do this. Your next first step is one of your hardest because this one calls for discipline.

Out of nowhere, one of your main hangout partners gives you a call and says that there is a party to end all parties coming up on Friday. You have a training session on Friday. Nothing new, just a plain nothing out of the ordinary training session to get you ready for a tournament. This would be the first time that you would have missed a training session.

You will make up for it by working out on Saturday. You decide to tell your friend no and still go to your scheduled Friday training. This is your first step towards being a champion because you have shown discipline and acknowledged to yourself that you would do what it takes to achieve your dream of being an elite fighter. This is the same level of discipline that you will use to be a success at anything else that you do in life.

As I have said, to get to where you want to be, you must start from where you are. I know some of you may think that statement makes no sense, but it does. Your destination does not impact your position, and neither does your position impact your destination.

If you have ever had physics, this will make sense. If you have ever had a class in philosophy, it will also make sense. But, if you have never had either, let me help you out and make it make sense.

(If you ever run across Mr. Schrodinger, say hello to his cat for me.)

Our natural state of being is stillness. We only move when we must move. We, humans, will sit, slouch, or lay in one spot all day if we don't have to work, use the bathroom, or eat. I personally have seen people sit at one place for an entire day only playing a video game. They would get up sporadically to use the restroom and grab something to eat, maybe.

Even when most people are not video game slugs, they will remain very sedentary. To change this, they must want something. This is your first of first steps, knowing why you are doing what you are about to do.

Most people start martial arts for one of three reasons. They want to: be healthy and get in shape; they want to learn self-defense, or they want to be a badass! A lot of people will deny this, but it is absolutely true.

They may have a reason other than the ones written here, but that is not the reason they walked into a gym. It is not the thing that got them to start. This is a major first step, understanding why you want to do it.

After they have found out what is going to motivate them to get into a gym or school, they then ask themselves, "Will I be good at this?" This is an easy one to answer, yes you will. Why? Because you are going to bust your butt to be not just good but better than the average person.

How are you going to do it? You are going to do it by investing time and energy into your pursuit. Of course, the next obvious question is what does *"good"* mean in martial arts?

Being good in any style means that you can perform the basic techniques of the style that you are studying and do them in a dynamic and confident fashion. It also means that you can and have used them in some sort of open combat way. For most of us, that will be in the form of sparring outside of our school.

This last part is essential. Why? You must move beyond your circle of safety. You will never know your potential until you interact with those outside of your small pond. You must dip your toes into the warm waters of the ocean and all the diversity that is there.

Another of your many first things is to realize that this is new to you, and it was new to every other person that you have met at your gym at one time. Like you, they all started doing pushups, jumping jacks, sit-ups, reverse punches, front kicks, and the list goes on until they got to wherever they were on the day that you met them. They stayed, they persevered, and they got better. You, hopefully, will be better than them and look good doing so.

The next first that is important: your first day of sparring! This was, for me, one of the most dreaded days that I had at school. Breaking boards gave me a h..d on! I loved doing drills. I adored hitting targets (bag work was my jam!!!). I enjoyed all of these things, but the first time I was scheduled to spar on the mat in front of everyone, I panicked.

I still remember it. My first school was Olympic Karate Studio's, and it was on the second floor of a building on the corner of Randolph and Dearborn. This was right in the heart of downtown Chicago. It was a Thursday evening. Sensei Michael Rivas told me that I would be one of the only low ranks there.

It would be me, a white belt girl named Sydnie, another yellow belt, one green belt, and everyone else would be blue and purple belts. A grand total of 16 people.

I had sparred but not in front of this many people before. Due to limited space, everyone sat down on the mat in a U shape. There was the center ref (sensei Rivas), two brown belts, two black belts all sitting on folded chairs, and the rest of us. The first two people got up and warmed up.

Each had a black belt speaking to them about what to do and how to do it.

Thursday and Friday were normally the last nights that the people who were going to fight on Saturday and Sunday would officially spar anyone. If you sparred on Thursday, you were fighting on Saturday and Friday; it was your turn on Sunday. You always had a day to relax; however, the bigger the fight, the longer your scale-down time was. For major tournaments, you had your last hard fight was a week before.

The first people up were a couple of purple belts fighting the two brown belts that were there. They both did round robin fighting to start, which means that each of them stayed on the mat until they had sparred everyone that was a purple or blue belt.

This was nonstop fighting until your opponent was switched out. That's 11 fighters, nine purple belts, and the last two brown belts who are ready to impress the Sensei. The rounds were 3 minutes each, more or less. The center black belt or Sensei would eyeball the time. It could be 3 minutes or 10 minutes. It was your job to be ready. Our cardio was on point back then.

After they finished going through what was great for me to watch, it became my turn to fight. We did almost the same thing, but it was the white belt first, the other yellow belt, me, the green belt, and the six lowest purple belts. The purple belts were there to learn control and movement. The rest of us were to be aggressive, use footwork, and practice basic techniques.

To make a long story short, I was horrible. Even Sydnie, the white belt and my future girlfriend (in my head), beat me. It was a disaster. I don't think that it could have possibly been worse than what it was. I was wrong. Little did I know, but my dad had talked to Sensei Mike about me fighting at a tournament that was going to take place that Saturday. It was going to be that Saturday. This would be another first step for me.

I licked my wounds and went home after talking to Sensei Mike about Saturday. He said he was confident that I would do well. He told me that I would only be fighting other yellow belts and that everyone that I saw would be just like me. This was the first out-and-out lie that he had ever told me.

I could not sleep a wink Friday night. I tossed and turned. When I got in my dad's car to go to the tournament, I was nervous and confused. Why was I doing this? Could I just bow out? What if we just went to McDonald's or the park instead of the tournament? My mind thought of hundreds of things I would have rather done then go to this thing.

As soon as we got there, I saw people who I knew from the dojo. This kind of calmed me down. The tournament was being held at a high school, which was and is still common. My dad and I went up to the register and signed in. My dad paid the money and signed the necessary papers.

I went to the restroom, and there seemed like there were a thousand guys changing into their gi's. When I came out and found my father, we went to the gym. I had died and went to martial arts heaven!

It was amazing. I saw people with weapons moving around and practicing. There were about 90 people doing different kata's, which at the time I thought were extraordinary and very mystical. Around the edges were groups of white, yellow, and green belts practicing with either black or brown belts or each other. The gym was set up into multiple rings.

Each ring had about 30 or 40 kids younger than me sitting on the floor watching one of their peers in the center of their circle doing a weapons or unarmed kata. I didn't know it then, but this is the way that I would see it done for the next 47 plus years.

I walked and hung around the other people from Olympic Karate Studios until I was told to get my equipment on and start warming up. I thought I had been nervous before. I was completely wrong. I found my dad and got my bag from him.

He had to have seen how nervous and scared I was. Once I retrieved my bag from him, I started to put first my safety kicks own, then my mouthpiece and my safety punches. I already had my cup in my jockstrap and my mouthpiece in and on.

At the time, I did not know that there was a strategy for how you arranged yourself to fight at tournaments. I had no clue as to what to do, even though I vaguely remembered being told just that morning what to do by Sensei. All of what he said went out the door as soon as they herded all of my kindred souls together.

They called all yellow and white belts to come together. Then they sorted us by age and size. We were all led to a ring, separated into two rows, and then bowed in front of a bunch of black belts which I had never seen before.

We were all commanded to sit on the ground in twos. I was in the first row. The guy in the row directly sitting behind me would be who I would fight.

We watched as each set of two got up and went to the center of the ring. When they got there, they would bow to the black belts first, the center judge, and then each other. He would ask them if they understood what was to happen.

They would nod in the affirmative. He would then place his hand between them as they stood on a piece of tape approximately 2 feet apart. He would lower his hand and say fight/start or something else. In this case, I believe it was Hajime.

I don't remember there being a clock or time being kept. I remember that you had to get a certain number of points. Once you got those points, you would be sent to an area to the side of the black belts. If you lose, you are free to go about your way. I watched five sets of two go up before it was my turn.

I vividly remember the center ref calling me and the kid behind me up to fight. He knocked on our cups, made us smile to check our mouthpieces, made us turn our palms up to make sure we didn't have long nails, and then told us to stand at attention. No one had headgear. I could see my father out of the corner of my eye. I could also hear several of our black belts yelling for me to pay attention.

My stomach was in knots. I thought I was going to puke. The next thing I know, I see a hand coming down and someone yelling Hajime. I wish I could say that I won this or the next couple of fights I went to, but I can't. This was my first loss. In fact, I loss the next four.

It wasn't until my fifth tournament that I acquired my first official win. This first led to others. Winning is habit-forming. The more you win, the more you want to win. However, to do this, you must continue to practice harder and smarter at every opportunity. These are the first steps in your journey to being an elite champion.

Chapter 6: A Brief History of Martial Arts

What we think of when we think of martial arts are the fighting arts that came from Southeast Asia. Europe, Africa, The Middle East, and the great subcontinent of India had martial arts also, but they failed to spread out far and wide as those from Eastern Asia did. Even worse than that, they failed to capture the imagination of the world.

When we talk about martial arts, we can say unequivocally that the oldest combat style is wrestling. Wrestling is the precursor to boxing. Every great nation in the world has or had some form of wrestling practiced by its ancestors. The Greeks of ancient Europe have wrestling praised in the "_Iliad._" India had the practice of Malla-yuddha (a form of wrestling.) In fact, the incredible book called the Mahabharata from the 5th century BCE talks about a famous warrior named Malay practicing it.

Martial arts were talked about as early as 1700 to 1100 BCE in what is now India. Like Buddhism, the martial arts that came from India started to morph, seed, flower, and grow. Fighting was intermingled with Taoist, Confucian, Shinto, and other philosophies that existed in their particular countries of origin. Later it would change the indigenous arts found in The Philippines, Thailand, Vietnam, Malaysia, Burma, and Indonesia and grow and disperse.

The native arts of The Philippines, Vietnam, and Indonesia are often given short shrift historically to their home-grown styles that were around several hundred years before what some call the Buddhist wave. Where Buddhism went, martial arts flourished. However, there are four that stand out in prominence.

The four countries that can claim to be progenitors of modern martial arts/sports and combat arts are China, Korea, Japan (starting in the Prefecture of Okinawa), and Thailand. An argument could be made for a fifth country, India. India is unique because of its diverse cultures and hegemony.

However, and I believe I can say this without any significant disagreement, Japan has had the most influence on modern combat training and martial sport. In fact, Japan cast a large and long shadow over modern martial arts in style, methodology, and type of technique. Clearly, the

Japanese influence can be felt. Its methodological influence in MMA is without a doubt.

Next is the drive and goal of perfection. I say China, i.e., Kung Fu, but I mean Bruce Lee. Without him, the modern point, full contact, and current gladiatorial blood sport known as MMA would not exist. An argument, I'm sure, could be made for the existence throughout the history of bloody one on one combat existing in every major epoch and country in history. England, France, Egypt, Nigeria, South Africa, Spain, Norway, and of course, America have had hidden or open and public fighting going on for centuries.

Before Bruce Lee modernized Kung Fu and transformed his version of it from Wing Chun to Jeet Kune Do, he popularized it on the big screen and turned it into a piece of violent but beautiful art. Because of Bruce Lee and his flashy Kung Fu, China was no longer the weak man of Asia.

They were a force to be reckoned with, envied, and emulated. Black kids on Chicago's Westside wanted to be like that short, possibly 135lb lean, mean wrecking machine. Bruce Lee symbolized cool, power, and dignity with a side order of nun chucks.

Korea is unique. Korea has given the world many things that are useful and wonderful; Taekwondo is one of its greatest gifts. Even with Japan's massive influence in martial arts, Korea has the most popular martial art in the world with Taekwondo. Taekwondo is the first martial art to be accepted as an Olympic sport since Judo.

Korea, known as the Middle Kingdom, is really the most modern of countries. The Republic of Korea, also known as South Korea, and the Democratic Republic of Korea, known as North Korea, did not come about until 1948 after the Japanese were defeated in World War II and forced to relinquish their now former colony. From 1910 to 1945, Korea was a colony of Imperial Japan.

Taekwondo, like Japan's Karate, is a very modern martial art. Korea, being a country either at war or on the brink of war with itself or a neighbor, has been on a high military alert for eons. Because of that, it has developed quite a few martial arts. Kwon pup and Subak are two of the most well-known styles that directly contributed to the development of modern Taekwondo. However, if we are looking for a more immediate impact on modern martial sports and fighting in general, we need only look at Thailand.

You cannot deny the impact that Thailand and its fighting style Muay Thai or Thai boxing, has had on the martial arts. You can see its influence on Bruce Lee and his development and technical strategy. Muay Thai has the aggression and strategy of Western boxing and kicking that Asian fighting arts are imbued with.

Let us go back to China for a moment. If there is a love for martial arts, it is epitomized and embodied in a human form. That form goes by the name of Bruce Lee! No one is more popular or famous in martial arts than he is. If he were alive today, he could claim to be the reason why MMA is what it is today.

No one person can claim to have gotten more people interested in the martial arts than him. More masters, instructors, athletes, competitors, and students will tell you that they got interested in the martial arts because of him than anyone or anything else. Having said that, there is one small little place that can say that it was the one that ignited the fire of fighting that we see now, and that place is Okinawa.

Okinawa is incredibly unique in that it is the place that created what we know now as Karate. Karate started as a fad and grew into something far more significant than could have been imagined just over a hundred years ago. Kara te is not empty hands but China hand to the Okinawans. Until karate was transferred to Japan, it had low kicks, grappling and was mainly a self-defense art. In fact, karate did not gain its high and often fancy kicks until it incorporated Savate (French foot fighting) into its arsenal. For a detailed explanation of this, check out the book "Asian Fighting Arts –

by Donn Draeger. For my money, this is the best book on martial arts are history.

This book is not about the history of martial arts. For now, the aforementioned "Asian Fighting Arts" is the best that I am aware of on the subject. However, there are plenty of sources online for those interested in a deeper dive into the subject.

I personally like the entertaining YouTube personality Jesse Enkamp also known as the Karate Nerd. If he's the nerd, This, of course, makes me the martial arts Geek!! There are, for the nerds like me, several very scholarly works out there. I encourage the serious student of martial arts to dive in and do some research.

All of the arts written about here owe a debt to India and the religious and philosophical underpinnings that flourished there and sprouted eastward. Most parents and even adult students comment on the sense of dignity, discipline, confidence, and morality centered that comes from learning a martial art. Students and practitioners, and even those that have nothing to do with it, comment on how martial arts training changes people for the better. Much of this can be attributed to the Buddhist roots that run deep in each of the four major art forms. All of this is because of a former Indian prince.

Chapter 7: Martial Arts Philosophy - Reasoning and Pragmatism

I love fighting, but at 60 years of age, there is not a lot of hard fighting that I can still do. The spirit is strong, but the flesh is weak. I now can appreciate the nuances of fighting, but more importantly, the philosophy behind the arts. The previous chapter was about the history of martial arts. Now we look at the philosophy behind that history.

We know the when; now, we look at the why and how. I want to know what is behind that curtain. The curtain in martial arts is the philosophy behind what we, as fighters, do. This chapter will look first at the ancient ideas and move towards the modern why. We are taking a very deliberate look and the path because it is important for today's fighters, point, full contact, and mma, to see what they do from a historical perspective.

Why did gladiators, fighters, warriors, and ancient athletes do what they did at the high caliber that they did things? What kept them going? What made them pass on their ideas and beliefs to their proteges and students? Why have their beliefs lasted for millennia?

There are many levels to the philosophy of martial arts. These levels are broken up into a multitude of ways. There are the original philosophical reasons as to why various styles have and do what they do. There is the modern ethos of today's point and mma fighters as to why they do what they do.

Some of the current philosophy of fighting is based on geography and the culture that the fighters have inherited. There are even sociological reasons, naturally, as to why fighters do what they do. This chapter will look at all of these factors and touch on them briefly.

A wiser and far more scholarly person than I will have to go into the details of all of this. For now, we will give you a very simple and cursory look and examination of the historical aspects of martial arts philosophy, along with a modern look at the current reasons and etymology of combat philosophy.

What we currently do in Karate, Jiu-Jitsu (Japanese and Brazilian), Kung Fu, Tae Kwon Do, and even in MMA has deep philosophical underpinnings. Most students never think about it or are even exposed to it, but combat arts are more than just throws and kicks. There are reasons behind what we do and even more for why we do what we do. As it is with anything that has lasted for hundreds or thousands of years, there exists a philosophical reason as to why that is.

It is commonly, and rightfully, acknowledged that martial arts, as we currently know it and recognize it to be, were started in India but blossomed in China. From there, it spread to all of South East Asia but mainly developed in the big three Japan, Korea, and Thailand. Each, as is commonly known, has its own martial arts philosophy that is particular to the individual styles and instructors, i.e., fighters, of those styles.

Humans being humans, like to make things their own. People want to see the world through their own eyes and their specific world views. We all like to give our own renditions of foods that we have discovered from other places. I want to cook my curries differently from the way my good friend Freddie Addae taught me. He is from Ghana, and there are very subtle differences between his taste and mine. I have a particular spin on things that he would not have. The same exists in martial arts.

All martial arts have a central core philosophy that is composed of harmony, peace, and respect for others. The first and key for and to the beginner, and it is the same in Kung Fu, Karate, Muay Thai, and Tae Kwon Do, is to defeat your opponent. The second is to be glorious in victory. Last and probably most important and essential to the warrior, but not necessarily to the athlete, are duty, country, tribe, and honor.

This last one, and we will talk about this several times in this book and this chapter, is to be an honorable person and to live our lives in an honorable way. The idea of honor is often talked about by athletes but only superficially so. There is substantial historical evidence behind this, but for now, we will point out only one part. For the martial artist, it is important to understand that you must forgive your opponent and try to empathize with why they did what they did. This is not true of the athlete, necessarily.

Universally it is understood that we must defeat our enemy. What differs from place to place is how we do this. Like in western boxing, most southeast Asian martial arts want to see a glorious battle! The technique that is used must be flawless and utilized with surgical dispatch. The parts of the body and how those parts are used in combat are very important. As a stellar example, we have Tae Kwon Do.

The Korean people are proud and very hardworking people. They are also very interested in appearances, and that is embodied in their love of literature, art, and the sub-genre of the fine arts. This will manifest itself in how they view body parts. Out of the southeast countries, Korea places a great deal of respect on the hands and the care thereof. The hands are viewed as things of beauty and are used to create art and literature. On the other end, literally, we have the feet.

The feet are made for toil and dirty work. Thus, we have Tae Kwon Do. Of the great martial arts, and Tae Kwon Do is one of them, no other style uses the feet, i.e., Tae Kwon Do, as much. Tae Kwon Do is known for its dominant use of the legs and, therefore feet, to fight. Why sully the hands, which are made to create beauty, when I can do the dirty work of defeating my opponent with my feet?

I realize that some will think that this is a stretch, and it just might be. However, it is firmly rooted in Korean sociological and cultural history. Even young Korean men and women view the hands as something to be cared for and pampered. Your hands are considered the pathway towards creating art and beauty. They are for learning and education. They are extensions of the mind. The feet for work and carrying loads.

For Tae Kwon Do, you get your greatest glory by doing something spectacular with your feet. Your most significant scoring opportunity is when you bring your feet from the ground and kick your opponent in the head with a decisive kick. Koreans, in order to imbue the feet with some dignity, look for a technique that is "superior in it is an execution" and use. I heard this over and over from master Choi at the Kukkiwon in South Korea. China has a similar idea about using the feet.

Most Kung Fu styles are very holistic. They look within for motivation. For the majority of Kung Fu styles, the philosophical underpinnings are not in Buddhism but Taoism (pronounced "*Dowism like a cow*"). The second influence is Confucianism. Both are very distinct and impact native philosophies that affect not just Kung Fu but most of Chinese history, family, and interpersonal/individual behavior. A clear example of the Taoist impact can be seen in some of the inner or softer styles of Kung Fu.

The colloquial term would be Wudangquan. This is a direct Taoist connection to Kung Fu as we know it now. The name may sound familiar to some ears. The Wudangquan, or Wudang style, is talked about in the international hit movie "***Crouching Tiger, Hidden Dragon***." The Wudang style is different from the Kung Fu of the northern Shaolin. Both are monks but separated by geography and philosophy.

The Wudang (also sometimes called Wu-Tang – (shout out to my boys of the Wu-Tang Clan: RZA, GZA, Ol' Dirty Bastard, Method Man, Raekwon, Ghostface Killah, Inspectah Deck, U-

God, and Masta Killa!) were internal or "soft" style fighters. Part of the larger Neijia or internal martial arts. The stylist followed a decidedly nonphysical way of training. Cultivating their chi and utilizing their spiritual faith were all part of making their techniques better.

Styles that are associated with Neijia are Baguazhang, Tai Chi Chuan, and Qigong. All have a very relaxed and loose way of moving. Movements, on the whole, are circular in both defense and attack. Their attacks and defenses are fueled by spiritual and mental energy.

Taoism was being practiced in China before Buddhism by a good measure. Truth be told, Taoism has firmer roots in Kung Fu (Wushu) than Buddhism does. It is transplanted as both a philosophical and religious foundation with the Shaolin monks later.

Lao-Tzu created Taoism somewhere in the area of 604-531 BCE. He famously wrote the '***Tao Te Ching***,' also called "the Tao." or when translated, "the Way." The Tao is a group of lectures, stories or parables, that show a person seeking enlightenment, how to move in harmony with your enemy, with yourself, and of course, with nature. When we talk about some of the universal concepts in martial arts, one of the first ideas outlined and set as a foundation is the idea of a man living in harmony.

Nothing in the world is softer and weaker than water;
But, for attacking the hard and strong, there is nothing like it!
For nothing can take its place.

*That the weak overcomes the strong, and the
soft overcomes the hard,
This is something known by all, but
Practiced by none.*

(Tao Te Ching, chapter 78).

As I mentioned before, I have distilled from my years of learning from so many people more intelligent and enlightened than I am a few concepts that I think are universal. Before we get to that, let us talk about three concepts that permeate the lore of martial arts and the warrior ethos.

These ideas are part of the universal warrior code that is embedded in the martial philosophy of South East Asia, and that is practiced in combat sports. These three ideas are central to almost all martial and military philosophies that I am aware of. Duty, honor, and forgiveness are.

Duty is essentially easy to define. When you have a duty to someone or something, i.e., country or agency, you have an obligation and responsibility to that person or thing. The strength of that obligation or responsibility is usually rooted in a religious or moral obligation. Whatever that sense of obligation and responsibility is tied to, the person that the duty is pinned to must believe in it strongly and with all of their being.

Most times, a person's sense of duty is tied to their religious beliefs. In Korea and Japan, historically, it was attached to fealty to a king, emperor, or religious beliefs. In China to Confucian rhetoric or, like the Japanese, imperial mandate. In either case, all three had external forces that linked the idea of duty to the individual.

The same process has worked its way into Western cultures. Duty to the military in various Catholic countries has been a powerful tool for centuries. European warriors have colonized various countries because it was their duty, as they saw it, to both country and church. A popular refrain by many military people is a duty, service to God, and country.

In our more secular times, warriors around the world still feel a sense of duty but believe that it comes from within. An agnostic or atheist still has to believe in something. There is still that human hunger to want to do right. I personally believe that we all have a desire to have a moral compass that not only drives us to do good things but guides us to do good things.

For the non-believer, that belief must come from within. Since there is no God or other outside deity to give them strength, they look inwards. In my opinion, and it is only my opinion, atheist and agnostics are far more fervent than their religious brethren. They must muster all their strength and lean on no one but themselves for the belief as to why they are obligated to believe that they have a duty to anything or anyone.

Honor is a more ephemeral concept. I cannot give you a clear definition, but I do have a list of its components. For our purposes, honor encompasses ethical behavior, morality, a sense of righteousness, high principles, honesty, integrity, and, for me, nobility. These are all things to strive for. Sometimes you will reach all seven parts of what it is to be an honorable man or woman.

Most times, you only attain three or four. I personally have failed to be as honorable in all aspects of my life as I would like, but as a warrior, I must continue to strive for perfection. This leads to another part of this idea, religious faith.

I liked to tell people that I am not a religious person, but I was raised in a religious house. It would have been impossible for certain things not to be learned and embedded in my view of the world and how I walk through it. I am not a Christian, but my grandparents were, and they raised me to be like them. I have read the bible and went to bible school as a youngster. While I am not an expert, I am passingly familiar with the ideas and concepts espoused in the bible. Due to this, I feel very comfortable with talking about certain parts of the bible.

There are several biblical sayings I will use here that have an impact on the ideas of duty, honor, and perseverance.

Do unto others as you would have them do unto you - Appearing in the Gospels of Matthew 7:12 and Luke 7:1, Jesus recommends that you try to treat others as you would like to be treated.

Judge not, lest you be judged - In Matthew 7.1, Jesus says not to pass judgment on others.

O ye of little faith! - When Jesus walked on water, he told Peter to come to him. Peter got out of the boat that he was in and walked on water until he realized what he was doing. At this point, he got scared and began to sink. Jesus advises us to have faith always, even in the middle of life's storms.

Love your neighbor as yourself - in Matthew 32:39 and Mark 12:3, Jesus told those that would listen to treat others with mercy, love, and compassion—the standard for all interaction with others.

An eye for an eye, a tooth for a tooth - Jesus in his Sermon on the Mount, which appears in Matthew 5:38-39, reminds all of us to forsake seeking revenge on those who have hurt you.

Turn the other cheek - Jesus gives the instruction, which appears in Matthew 5:39 and Luke 6:29, that discourages us from seeking revenge.

In the Quran, we have: The Prophet Muhammad showed great mercy when he forgave Washi, the criminal who murdered and mutilated his uncle Hamza. "O My Devotees, who have committed excesses against their own selves, do not despair of the mercy of Allah. Surely, Allah forgives all sins. Indeed, He is the Most Forgiving, Merciful" (Quran 39:54). We then learn, "And the recompense of evil is punishment like it, but whoever forgives and amends, he shall have his reward from Allah; surely He does not love the unjust" (Quran 42:40).

Forgiveness is a key component to being a civilized individual that lives in a civilized society. The idea of forgiveness is a central idea in Christianity, Islam, Judaism, and Buddhism. At the end of every war and the end of every competition, the warrior and the competitor must be able to forgive the transactions of those that they have faced.

In fact, duty and honor are of no good if one cannot forgive. You cannot move on with your life and your relationships; if you cannot forgive, you cannot continue with enjoying the world and the wonderful life that it offers each one of us.

As a warrior or fighter, I must forgive my enemy/competitor eventually. We cannot continue to fight. Ultimately there will be a physical victor, and if it is them or me, I must learn to forgive them for the trespasses of the past and build a new future where the two of us, our families, friends, and countrymen and women, can move forward in a productive and joyful way.

The warrior, and even a combat athlete, must have guidelines to work and live by. Historically all of us have sought out philosophies to make our lives better. The military and the martial (military/fighting) arts have been one avenue that many have used to do this. I, personally, have used the martial arts and the ideas intrinsic to them to give me meaning and a way of moving through my day-to-day life. It has made me a better person even when I have failed to do the right and honorable thing.

Buddhism and Confucianism (in China and parts of Korea) are intrinsically built into the southeast Asian countries that the bulk of modern martial arts come from. Buddhism, however, is the core in most of the modern iterations of the philosophical parts of martial arts philosophy.

This book may be aimed at combat athletes, but it also speaks to military men and women. For the combat athlete, we have clear tenants that can be applied to other sports but have a certain precision to what we do.

- **Be fair.** The ultimate goal is to see who is better trained. That can't be done by cheating.

- **Be a good sport.** You are not enemies in the ring. You are competitors. Shake hands and part as friends always.

- **Try your best.** You will never know what you can do unless you do your best.

- **Strive to be better mentally and physically every day.** Your real competition is who you were yesterday.

For the warriors:

- **Defend** your family, friends and teammates.

- **Always** exhibit the best qualities of your country.

- **Maintain** your weapon, equipment, and body to be able to perform at the highest levels needed for combat.

- **Always** strive to do the honorable thing. If you fail at this, apologize, and dedicate yourself to righting any wrong(s) that you may have caused by your actions.

- **Duty** comes before any personal gains.

- **Do** the right thing even when it countermands a direct order.

- **Always** be kind and defend the weak and downtrodden. The strong should never take advantage of the weak.

- **Defend** your country, its citizens, and treasures zealously and honorably.

This next part of the chapter is more about what we believe philosophically in martial arts. In particular in how we train, who we train, and the mindset of modern martial training.

People often forget what martial arts are for. In fact, calling what we do martial arts, in general, is a misnomer. We are engaged, again in general, in fighting arts and not war (martial) arts or ways.

People are in such a hurry to call themselves warriors that they forget that warriors use weapons and are looking for ways to kill others.

Ninety-eight percent of the people that take martial arts are civilians and are looking only to defend themselves from attackers. For a treatise on this, look at the history of pre-Karate fighting methods of feudal Japan. Farmers and peasants only wanted to protect themselves and their families.

Civilians do not go and look for fights. Warriors do. A civilian doesn't care what an opponent will do in the hour after they have fought. A military person does. People know what soldiers and warriors do. One thing that they often forget is that they know how to retreat. You do so in an orderly way, but you do it with great haste and much zeal. In Chicago, when you are running, you call it hauling ass. It's my favorite technique and has worked successfully for me for years now.

The greatest joy that an instructor can ever have is when one of their students comes back to the dojo/school/gym and tells them how they were able to deescalate a situation and that they didn't have to fight at all. Yes, I am ecstatic if they tell me that the training that they received from me allowed them to kick some butt, but avoiding the fight altogether is even better.

I take a great deal of time and energy in teaching "nonfighting" fighting. This was primarily for my students who had reached puberty and up. For me, and it is part of my personal philosophy, avoiding conflict is as important as knowing what to do when you must be part of it.

A few years ago, a student told me about how he was able to deescalate a situation. He was at a place with some people that he didn't really know. Cards were being played, and one of the people that he was playing cards with said that he was cheating. One thing led to another, and he was pinned up against a wall. He didn't say he was a black belt or say he would rip someone's head off. He made a joke that he had heard from Dave Chappelle, and the guy laughed and calmed down.

My student gathered himself, laughed, and left. That night, laughter was better than a sidekick or a right cross. Of the many ways that he could have fought this person, the technique of humor is what prevented a fight and possibly saved his life. I tell you this story to point out that fighting is not always the answer.

This is often the basis for most martial arts philosophy, avoid fighting. I would say that fighting should always be the last answer. In point of fact, I would say that this is what martial arts teach at its core. Live, love, laugh, and learn as much as possible, but fight only when there is no other choice.

The martial arts are a metaphor for life. Fighting teaches us that if we work hard, are diligent in the study of fighting that we can transcend some of our pettiness and reach a certain level of enlightenment. If we work on our form and practice how to apply it repeatedly, we then know that we can be something better than what we started off as. If, when we go into battle, we can face it, unafraid and calm, unlike when we began, we have changed ourselves for the better.

As a fighter, you and I must face the trials, tribulations, pain, and death that possibly awaits us every time we go into the ring or battle. For us, each battle is an opportunity to face first fear, then death. Every reverse punch, spinning back kick, elbow, or chokehold, slowly reveals the face of death to us.

The way of the warrior, no matter how you name it, has certain characteristics but clear goals. These goals are the same no matter what country, century, race, or ethnicity the way comes from. We talked earlier about universal truths in martial arts. The only thing that really varies is how. Each of us takes a different path to the top of the mountain, but we all can eventually get there.

Point competition is just that, a competition. In martial arts, it is special because it is a training exercise and a guide for instructors. It is not the purpose of martial arts! If you are looking for this to be a yardstick for someone's ability to defend themselves on the street, you are looking at the wrong tool. However, in the dojo/gym/ring, it can be, but only if it is open to all.

Traditionally, in Japan, China, and Korea, martial arts are taught separately for the two sexes. As I mentioned earlier, harmony is a universal core in martial arts philosophy. In my view, men on one side and women on the other take us out of harmony. Training this way is also very patriarchal.

However, in recent years in places like the USA, Europe, and Africa, we are seeing training become slightly more egalitarian and equal. This ultimately means that martial training should be in more of an open-pit environment which allows for not just better training but fairer training. I should add that fairer training means better training. Of course, this brings us to the question of: "Why is this important anyway?"

Women are attacked by men more. Bigger boys and girls attack little boys and girls. If you are a woman or a man and you want to defend yourself against a potential male rapist, you have to practice fighting with adult men. If you are a little boy or girl, you must practice fighting big boys and girls.

This is where the military (martial) philosophy around training comes into self-defense. Soldiers do not get better by training against those that are the same or weaker than they are. They get better by going against someone who is the same size or bigger than their potential opponent. Of course, this does not necessarily apply to combat sports where you have weight, gender, and age classifications.

If a person is taking martial arts and they are a woman or child, they should never be segregated on their workouts. This is especially true when they have joined a class for self-defense. The reason why is that they have to get used to defending and fighting those that will be their attackers. Women should only be in a class that consists of all women for exercise and full contact (mma) fighting. Never, never, ever for self-defense.

Concerning mma, it does not have a strong philosophical bent it. Like boxing, it does not have to involve itself with philosophy and issues of morality. MMA and boxing make no claims to making better humans by teaching them to fight and kill, as is done by the more popular martial arts, i.e., karate, Taekwondo, Hapkido, and kung fu. According to some fighters, the only thing that is important is fighting. I disagree with that part.

At this point, I should bring up the fact that one of the things that the founders of modern MMA used to say is that weight and size meant nothing. In a truly pragmatic response, the only thing that matters is if the techniques or method works.

If it cannot knock an opponent out or make them submit, I don't need to learn it. I live in a city; why do I need to learn how to use a sword or staff? Nunchaku, swords, sai's, and most South and Southeast Asian weapons and North American weapons, for that matter, cannot be carried around by most people legally. If I cannot use it on the street, why should I learn it?

Before I go further, let me say that fighting is fighting. You fight with your mind, body, and spirit. The best and greatest fight with all three. Now they may only use a small part of their arsenal, but that small part is deadly and superior to most mortal folk. You also do not have to have any idea of the philosophical aspects of fighting to be great!

Let me just mention a few folks who may look normal but who are not. For example, Vasyl Lomanchenko (boxing – WBO featherweight Champion) and Steve Lopez (TKD – Olympic Gold medal winner) are both gifted on a level that most people will never understand. Both are incredible athletes and have garnered a great deal of success in their lives. Neither of these great athletes and fighters comes from a training regimen that was infused with a Taoist, Buddhist, or Prussian military education.

Vasyl Lomanchenko is a ring general in boxing. He comes in confident and always ready. Like any soldier, he trains hard all the time. Yes, he is strong, but not the strongest. Yes, he is fast, but not the fastest. What makes him worth mentioning is that he is smarter than almost everyone that he fights.

When he prepares to fight, he pictures the person that he is going to battle with. This is where his game plan starts to take form. Like a lot of high-caliber fighters, he pictures the fight, each punch, block, and counter, before he gets in the ring. He has had the fight already hundreds of times before they have even made their way into the ring. He sometimes knows his opponents' moves before they do.

He pays attention to details. How will they launch a hook after they have thrown a jab? What angle does he have to be to hit them in the liver after they have thrown a right cross? Lomanchenko knows these things, and like any great general, he has several plans on how to take advantage of the situation.

Steve Lopez is an Olympic gold medalist in Tae Kwon Do and a gifted natural athlete. Two things that rarely come together, a natural AND gifted! Steve has an older brother, Jean, who is a beast. To make it worse for athletic families everywhere that thought that they were it, he also has an Olympic caliber sister and younger brother!

As we have already mentioned, Steve Lopez is natural AND gifted. On top of these two great things, he is intelligent and well-trained. If I am not mistaken, he started training from his brother Jean, around the age of 5 or 6, in the family garage. For most people, this is way too young unless it's in wrestling or jiu-jitsu. For Steve, it was just at the right time.

First, he had the natural inclination, as discovered by his brother, for fighting. Next, he was found to be a natural athlete. Lastly, Steve is a smart guy. He watches other fighters. He studies them, and like Lomanchenko, he trains accordingly. Most importantly, as we will say repeatedly, he makes the sacrifices that it takes to be a champion.

Being a great fighter and martial artist comes down to being smart and working harder than your opponent. You do not have to know who Confucius was, nor know who Emmanuel Kant was. Understanding the philosophical aspects will make a fighter a better person all around. With an intellectual understanding of fighting and history, you become a champion in life.

Chapter 8: Mysticism, Bullshido, and Martial Arts

The martial arts have a lot of stories and fairy tales that are espoused as truths, but on even a cursory examination are clearly not true. Some of the stories are entertaining. The "Kung Fu" movies of the late '60s and '70s are full of action, with martial artists flying through the air and punching through walls with the greatest of ease. Stories of mystical powers that are hidden from the common fighter abound even to this day. This chapter is about this and why it is wrong.

One goal that every teacher should have is to prepare their students for the real world. You do that by telling them the truth about what you are training them to do. You root that training in things that make sense and that have been proven to work. You explain to them the how's and why's of fighting. You also dispel any myths that they may have heard about from others or from movies and wives-tales. In order to do this, you must use facts and reason.

There are certain laws of physics and mechanics that will help you explain the why and how of the success of a technique. There are certain scientific principles that cannot be circumnavigated because we believe that our chi will make it so. Bricks and boards are broken due to physics and not by concentration and focus of one's chi.

The same can be said for why and when certain types of techniques are used. A lot of them are very spectacular and flashy but have no place in a fight. Before we get to the unnecessary methods, let's address the issue of mysticism in the arts in the form of so-called internal energy, sometimes Qi/Chi/Ki/prana.

As the story goes, Qi/Chi/Ki/prana is part of a person's life force. It is said to be a vital force that all humans have in them that can be tapped into with the right training and focus.

Unfortunately, it has never been directly observed or studied independently by a scientist. According to certain martial artists, Chi is an energy unlike what physics is aware of supposedly. However, I will emphatically say that energy is all chi is. There is confusion and misunderstanding of what the word is trying to explain.

In the old days, back when I was young, instructors tried to explain how boards, bricks, bats, and bottles were broken with such ease. Chi is what prevented the person using it from breaking bones or tearing of skin and limbs. Ki allowed them to perform many incredible things. What was happening was that physics was being utilized. The masters and grandmasters tried to explain things to the best of their abilities.

Unfortunately, they were very confusing. Due to this inarticulate explanation, many students were led to believe in the supernatural. Martial arts have lots of myths and stories that are thought of as being facts. It, unfortunately, can be full of Bullshido. These stories are just not true. They are myths and misinterpretations of physical phenomena. They are entertaining but nevertheless wrong.

Fake martial arts stories create fake martial arts styles and, therefore, fake martial artists. Super-duper 15th-degree grandmasters who have fought Shaolin ninja monks. Standing 15 feet away from you, with their backs turned, they can knock you out with the power of their Qi and impregnate your grandmothers' pet goat. Often, they refuse to fight any well-known fighter because they may hurt or kill them. When they do fight them, they usually get beat to a pulp.

For us to understand why something is, we must study it and utilize tools that will allow us to discover the true nature of the thing being examined. We use science and reason. These tools have helped to take the world out of darkness, superstition, and unnecessary misery.

In fact, the last two centuries were brought about because of science and reason. Physics, chemistry, electronics, medicine, and technology are the children of reason and science. They have proven to work so well because of a process called the scientific method. What is the scientific method, you might be asking yourself?

The scientific method has six parts to it. First up is observations. This means keeping your eyes open and looking at the world. Number two is creating a question based on something that you have observed. As an example, I have observed that ants like sugar. I see them carrying it away every time that I waste it at my job. My question would be, why do ants like sugar so much?

Number three is to create a hypothesis. A hypothesis is a proposed answer to the question that you had about what you observed. To prove the hypothesis, you then put together an experiment to verify that the theory is correct. Finally, you finish the experiment and examine and analyze the data and come up with a conclusion.

A key part that I did not mention is that the experiment has to be one that can be replicated. Someone else should be able to come up with the same results if your experiment was put together properly and your hypothesis was logical. The ability to replicate is a significant reason why science has been such a success at making the world a better and more efficient world and is the defining part. I believe that the scientific method is here to help modern martial arts.

We, as martial artists, and in particular traditional martial artists, sometimes observe things that we know, in all, probably are not going to be used in a real fight. Nevertheless, and undoubtedly, it will not be the reason for a knockout. We also can be reasonably assured that our chi will not defend you or assist in taking out an assailant. We are modern men and women and, as such, need to teach our students and athletes practical and battle-tested methods of combat.

There is no such thing as dim mak (death touch), and we should not be telling students that. Chi/Ki is not real. You are never, ever going to knock someone out by hitting one of their pressure points. None of this mumbo jumbo is good for us, or the arts and styles that we practice and love. If there is something that you have a question about or you have some doubts about, use the scientific method.

Let us start with a technique that is used in almost every style that I am aware of. It is the spear hand. This technique calls for the defender/attacker to bring their fingers together under the middle finger tightly. The hand should resemble a spear, as the name implies. With enough practice and the development of calluses around the tip of the middle finger, one should be able to pierce the opponent's skin. Without fear of contradiction, I can boldly say two things.

First, no one that is reading this has ever seen or known anyone that has done this. At least in real life. You or a friend may have seen it in an old kung fu movie, but not in real life. Secondly, outside of using the technique to pierce wooden armor, during a battle in feudal Japan, when would you use it?

I am not a formal student of Brazilian Jiu-jitsu, but I do admire their more scientific approach to practice. A good buddy recommended that I check out a few of them, and I did. Two were traditional, and three were BJJ. The main difference between them was that with the BJJ schools, there is an emphasis on competition.

They worked a lot of mma style techniques, and some techniques were practiced without a gi at one of the schools. The two traditional schools spoke a little Japanese and did everything in gi except for the one day that they practiced self-defense.

What they had in common was that neither believed in some type of internal power. All worked on breathing and concentrated on perfect form and good technique. In point of fact, all of the Jiu-Jitsu schools, and there were five of them, placed great emphasis on techniques and repetition. However, there was a huge difference in the number of techniques learned.

The traditional Japanese schools took longer to promote to black belt because there were way more techniques to learn. Why because there was more emphasis on history and understanding why and how before they became black belts. Part of me likes the idea of the history associated with the how and why. The Brazilian Jiu-Jitsu schools were, on the other hand, emphatic about using techniques and training their students in techniques that they whole-heatedly believed that worked because they had tested them out in modern scenarios.

Two of the BJJ black belts told me that they went through the myriad of techniques that they taught and did an audit of them periodically. A group of them got together and tested them out, and asked others if they had the same experience with them. If they agreed that it worked, they kept it. If the majority said no, it was gone. They didn't just keep it because someone said it worked 200 years ago in one situation in a battle in some village that no longer exists.

I am a big fan of science and facts. I like the saying "trust but verify." Scientists say this every day. What makes science, and in turn scientist, so cool is that science requires that you do not just take someone's word about something or listen to tales of wonder, but that you question statements.

You trust that what they say is correct, but you test it out to be sure. Science requires doubt, questioning, and the relentless search for facts. The same exists with martial arts.

Chapter 9 - Fighters and Martial Artist

People that go into a dojo, or gym, will ultimately fall into two distinct categories. They are either fighters or martial artists. They never realize it, but they do. Sometimes they will fluidly move between the two. They will stay in one category and, without knowing it, move to the other and be just as comfortable with it as they were just moments before.

Fighters like the competition. They love the idea and feel of battle, either in the form of competition or on the battlefield. For them, it must be practical and no-frills. This group is usually (not always!) jocks, younger, male, fit, and like the adulation that comes from fighting and winning.

Jocks and former jocks like to dip their toes into the fight game at various points in their lives. Fighters, however, are also people who were formerly bullied or are still being bullied. They want to right the wrongs that happened to them or those that they identify with.

A considerable number of guys who were thought of as being effeminate are part of this group. This particular group is also sometimes the most aggressive in later life. They are also, sometimes, the most ardent when it comes to beating up perceived bullies.

Fighting gives you immediate feedback and almost instant gratification. Speak to someone who is a combat competitor, and they will often talk about the "high" that they get from fighting. They love the rush that they feel, even when they lose, of going one on one with an opponent. All that work and effort pay off in the end, with some type of battle. The sacrifices made for just those few minutes of battle and the thought of what they are going to do to their opponent sometimes gives them a feeling that cannot be duplicated anywhere else.

Fighters are also where the soldiers and marines come from. They are taught the tools and sent into battle. The ancient "berserkers" and "vandals" come from this line of fighters. They are the ones that stories are told about and songs are sung about. Their lives are short but made for glory. Martial artists are not necessarily interested in the battle, or at least not the endgame of it. Fighting for them is sometimes an afterthought.

Martial artists enjoy the training, strategy, and learning about the tools of fighting. They enjoy the history and, most importantly, the cultural aspects of it. They understand the details and minutia along with the whys and how's. They know how to gauge what the other fighter has, how, what and when to use a particular technique. Here is where you find the officers, coaches, and instructors.

In boxing, you have the great coach Angelo Dundee. He is most famous for being the coach of Muhammad Ali and Sugar Ray Leonard. He is, without a doubt, one of the greatest combat arts/martial artists to have ever lived.

His knowledge of boxing was encyclopedic. While never a competitor, he knew not only how to spot talent but how to turn them into champions. He understood what the tools of a fighter were and how they could be implemented.

When you look at the history of fighting, there are few fighters who have gone on to be a coach, let alone be a great coach. Why is this? One reason is the psychological part of the game. Next is the vision that you need to be a coach. Lastly, there must be a reward of something more than money to be a great fighter.

A good coach/instructor is like a good admiral or general. There is a certain mindset you must have for each of these roles. You must have a clear vision, and that vision must be part of a step-by-step plan. They are not just thinking about the next fight, but the next few fights. There must be a desire to create and mold things with a coach/instructor.

Fighters are primal and in-the-moment creatures. The only plan that they have is to kick their next opponent's butt. They train only for the next battle and not for the one afterward. Fighters have tunnel vision, and coaches have VISION! This is the way that it should be.

When the fighter is in the fight, that is where they should be. However, they also, in between rounds, must listen to their coaches and trainers. The coach sees what is happening in real-time. The fighter only sees what is in the moment and nothing else. To use a Star Wars metaphor, there is the master, and there is only one apprentice. The same paradigm exists in martial arts.

Chapter 10 - The New Covid-19 Landscape

When I started writing this book, there was no such thing as Covid19. In the spring of 2019, I was pleasantly oblivious of it or the idea of anything like it raising its ugly head in the possible future. March of 2020, and there it is. Not just a tiny innocuous version of the flu, but a full-fledged pandemic. A pandemic that has killed, as of this writing, more people than the Spanish flu of 1917 did.

Covid19 has wrecked lives and economies everywhere that it has landed. Athletics of all types have been hobbled. Combat sports and point competition, in particular, have been significantly impacted. Change in how we do things is essential. The real question that has to be answered is how?

Let us start with the low-hanging fruit when it comes to the coronavirus and safety for our students and athletes. Wash your hands with soap and warm water often. Many of us are used to doing this after a workout, but it is important that it is also done prior to hitting the mat or floor. Use an antibacterial soap and lotion when possible. If you cough, cough into the crook of your arm.

This one is hard for people like me but avoid shaking hands and hugging. Clean all contacted surfaces, with a disinfectant, areas that you or others have touched within an hour of it happening. The following is another hard one for me and most people I know, avoid touching your face. In particular, the nose and eyes. These are the easy things to do. Now for the more challenging part.

I have no concrete solution as to how fighters will work around this problem, but I do have some ideas to lessen the pain. Most specifically, with point fighting, which of course, is what this book is about. Ideally, everyone would arrive 14 days early, be screened by a doctor, then be placed in a bubble of a secure hotel or other safe lodging. From there, they would go directly, by a safe and managed bus, to tournament and fight. That is unlikely to happen.

This is not a be-all or end-all solution, and to be honest, it is only a small idea that will have to be experimented with and tested throughout the martial arts community. I am sure that eventually, the world will come out of this, but until then, competitors might have the opportunity to fight, learn and grow just as they have in the past.

The first thing is that schools will have to work together in groups. My recommendation is that they will do so by geographic closeness. For most schools, this is being done already. Most instructors I know are friends with or know intimately at least four or five senior students and their instructors or coaches at every school/gym within an hour's drive of where they are. They know these folks because they see them at tournaments, and as humans do, develop relationships with them.

Each school will submit the names, telephone numbers, and critical categorization information for the sponsors of the tournament that their students/athletes will be competing at.

The sponsors of the tournament will find a coronavirus testing facility and provide the telephone number and address of the facility to each and every competitor at least three weeks prior to the day of the competition.

Competitors must go to and submit themselves to be tested a minimum of twice within that three-week period. They will then be required to present a signed statement confirming the results of the test. This statement will be given to the tournament's sponsor on the day of registration for the contest.

On the day of the tournament, each fighter will always wear a mask in the area of competition. I recommend a modified full-face shield that would replace the nose/mouth covering or a helmet that has a mask built into it. Each competitor, before competing, will have all equipment, except for the mouthguard, groin protector, and chest guard that is beneath the uniform, sprayed with a sanitizing spray.

The fighters will be put in pools of eight per sex/weight/rank category, with no more than eight schools per grouping. This allows for a standard bracketing system of elimination that most schools are used to anyway. This will also keep the numbers of competitors down, but potentially, the quality of fighting up. Why? Because schools will only be able to have their most valued and deserving students competing.

Each school is allowed no more than ten students at any event, from white belt to green. From blue to brown/red, there is no limit. All competitors must register, with payment, no later than three days prior to the tournament. They must have had one negative test for Covid19 within 48 hours of the competition from a community-recognized testing facility.

All of the participating schools must agree to who and where testing is done. I would wholeheartedly advise the tournament sponsors to put together a list of doctors and facilities for the schools and individuals who register for the tournament ahead of time.

All schools must receive a visit by at least one authorized black belt from a school within their competition grouping. For those that have less than ten, their competitor will receive a bye until they reach even with whatever is the average number of competitors for their division

Competition has several components to it in most tournaments. There is a big reason why everyone is there, fighting, but there are two other categories. First are weapons, and next is kata or forms. Depending on where you live, weapons competition will have two components to it.

First is the traditional format of just fighting, as it is in most kata competition, swinging your weapon in the air at an imaginary opponent. The other is cooler and more in line with history, and that is a battle against an opponent who also has a weapon!

The latter is still very rare but is awesome if you can do it in a safe environment. If this is the case, it is an easy one to do. Solution: wear full body armor created by Chiron Global. This armor allows full-contact fighting with modified traditional weapons. The armor can also be easily be adapted to prevent against covid. As of now, it is expensive, but if competitors and sponsors have this as an option, I highly recommend it.

If anyone is seriously thinking about this, I would suggest that a few schools get together and buy in bulk to lower the price or pay for them to come to the USA, Canada, Mexico, or Western Europe was in Australia a few years back and saw a demonstration of it, and it was terrific. After weapons, the next category is formed/kata.

I hate kata! Let me take that back. Hate is too strong of a word. I do not hate kata. I'm just not a fan of it. Kata is like high school algebra or calculus to me. Teachers told me that it was good for me, but I could never think of how I would use it as an adult.

Kata and calculus were painful and caused much consternation in my young life. Now I see the light, or at least I do with kata. Before I get to my solution for kata, let me present an alternative for how kata should be judged and viewed in the near future.

As a citizen scientist and professional geek, I love data and technology. I like finding ways to use science and technology to improve efficiency. Science and technology are only tools. These tools, like all tools, are around to make human life more accessible, more efficient, and better. Kata, in my worldview, is an easy one to apply this to.

I must preface this by saying that what I am proposing is new and very different from what most of us are used to seeing and doing currently. It will take time to get used to this new way of doing things. First, kata is performed in front of 4 or more judges.

They usually sit in a row, side by side. The judges, if they have been around for a long time and are in the same system that the kata is performed in, know what the competitor is doing and why. Usually, if they are new judges, they have no idea of what they are looking at.

We propose several new things. First, before the competitor starts their kata, they provide the judges with a written bunkai of the kata. What is bunkai? The word bunkai means analysis or breakdown. It is the what and why of a kata. When a student does an uppercut after she did a kick, bunkai explains why that happened. For more detail what bunkai is and why it can be beneficial, check out https://www.karatebyjesse.com/kata-bunkai-omote-ura-honto/,

To assist the judges, we recommend something slightly new. In some places, this is being done, to some extent, already. We propose that for every kata competition, a written bunkai is presented from each competitor prior to starting their performance. Next, instead of the judges being directly in front of the competitor, that they are in a separate room/area viewing the kata from 5 camera angles. Front, left, right, rear, and from the top.

For the instructor that is a student of the style and a judge, this provides all the data that they need to confirm the bunkai. For the person that is the artist, the esthetics of the technique become clearer. The process, unfortunately, is longer, but since there are fewer people, they now have more time to judge. Another option for the judges, I would recommend, is to announce kata winners the next day or at the end of the tournament, after the fighting is over, instead of before.

Kata, as I am sure you know after my proposal, are pre-arraigned movements and techniques. They are performed in such a way that has the practitioner, theoretically, fighting an invisible opponent. At the center of every kata is the goal of making the fighter better.

According to my instructors, you master the technique and develop muscle memory so that when you are in actual combat, you are able to react and utilize your technique the way that it was meant to be used for our circumstances. My belief is that every battle is different, and so should every kata. This is wrong. Why? To make kata effective, we have to change how the kata is utilized.

In most styles' students learn a series of kata that are meant to propel them forward. The practitioner is looking to develop balance, speed, and strengthen techniques. For me, kata, at least now, is shadow boxing set in a disciplined pattern.

Masters of various styles have designed kata for their students that meet the fighting philosophy of their styles. Modern coaches want their fighters to be good or better than those of the past. Kata can, in my new world view, help them do that.

To do that, fighting coaches must have an idea of what they want their fighters to learn and how they want them to react. Forms must be designed for defense and attack. One way of doing this is to tell the fighter to create a kata to meet a particular criterion. For example, say to the fighter that they are going to fight two people. One person is about their height and weight, and the other is a little taller but considerably heavier. Then ask them what they would do and with what techniques.

With this, the coach will be able to see what techniques the fighter likes to use. Next, he will be able to get a fair idea of what the fighter thinks are targets to aim for. On the second go-around, because we are training a point fighter, the coach will tell the fighter to use what he or she is weak at. For example, if they only use sidekicks to bridge the gap, have them use a roundhouse kick.

The goal will be to have them use techniques that they either need to sharpen or that you want them to learn. After all, that is partially what kata is for. It is a fun and dynamic way of practicing techniques. It is dynamic, and because it is repetitive, it aids in developing muscle memory.

Most of the things listed here are simple and easy to do. The key to staying healthy in the age of covid is distance and using disinfectants. Working drills, pad work (while covered), and improvised kata will go a long way in keeping your fighter strong and ready when the time comes for sparring and ultimately ready for the championship fight.

Before we close, and as a brief reminder, these are the basic things that you should be doing anyway.

- Wash your hands regularly

- Avoid touching your eyes, nose, and mouth

- When you cough, sneeze into your elbow or a tissue.

- Disinfect and clean areas often that you frequently touch

Chapter 11: The Olympics and Martial Arts Competition

The Olympics were created initially to honor the gods of the ancient Greeks. Every year they sent athletes to other cities to pay homage to the gods. Citizens and athletes venerated the gods every year by performing to their very best to impress the god that was the patron of their city. No was more than the king of the gods, Zeus. The city of Olympia also held games, but they were every four years.

Olympia was named after the home of the gods, and naturally, Zeus, the king of the gods, was honored the most. The games held at Olympia were held every four years instead of every year as the other games were held. This gave the games there an added aura of specialness. This level of specialness called for only the best to come to Olympia.

The Greeks loved track and field, and the first Olympic games, which were held in 776 BCE, demonstrated that. They also loved fighting. Unlike their "uncivilized" Roman cousins, the Greeks hated gladiatorial fighting. That is not to say that they did not like conflict.

They were slow to warm up to it. They first started with wrestling being added to the Olympics in 708 BCE. Twenty years later, the real action started with boxing in 608 BCE. Lastly, Pankration made its debut in 648 BCE.

Pierre de Coubertin brought the Olympics back and opened it up, not for just the Greeks, but to the world in 1896. When they came back, with the exception of wrestling, there were few martial arts, and when they did, they were mainly demonstration sports. Boxing made a comeback at St. Louis, MO Olympic games in 1904. Unfortunately, no Pankration. It wasn't until the 1964 Tokyo Olympics that Judo was introduced as our new martial sport in the modern era.

At the 1988 Seoul Games, Taekwondo was an Olympic demonstration sport. At the 2000 Sydney Games, it became a medal-earning sport. It continues to be a very popular event at the Olympics and has an enthusiastic fan base. Unfortunately, it has very mediocre ratings from an advertising standpoint.

Personally, I believe that they should get rid of some of the guidelines that allow only certain types of techniques and only allow points for level of technical difficulty and not offensive acumen. The older, more deadly competitive rules for taekwondo should be reinstated. It would be more exciting and makes the art more practical. This brings us to our newest Olympic martial art, Karate.

Karate will start as an Olympic sport at the next Tokyo Olympics. It will follow the guidelines and philosophy of the World Karate Federation. It will recognize only the styles of Wado-Ryu, Shotokan, Goju-Ryu, and Shito-Ryu, all of which are part of the significant traditional styles found in the last 100 years of what is now considered conventional Japanese martial arts. I view them as what people think of when they think of karate from the movies. They are also styles recognized and promoted by the Japanese Karate Association (JKA).

The Olympic version of Karate sparring is very similar to what would have been seen back in the late 80's and early 90's point tournaments. The way fighters bounce and move. The mental philosophy of "one shot, one kill" translated into "one punch, one kill" still exists. The idea of knocking out an opponent with one punch still exists.

The most popular "traditionalists" are mma fighters like Lyota Machida (Shotokan), George St. Pierre (Kukushkin), Anderson Silva (Taekwondo), Anthony Pettis (Taekwondo), Ronda Rousey (Judo), and Stephen "Wonderboy" Thompson (Kempo).

This is not the end-all and be-all list, but it will suffice. Everyone here represents the idea of the one-hit one kill philosophy. This is the fighting philosophy that will be exhibited at the Olympics.

When karate comes to the games, we will see something definitely different from taekwondo. There will be more balance with the kicking and striking. This will be the closest that we will come to having a martial artist fighting that we will get until we have some sort of a mma/pankration style of fighting in the Olympics.

As of the time that I write this, I do not believe that the equipment will have any sort of sensors built into them as there is in the bodyguard in Taekwondo for scoring. There will be just two fighters and a center referee.

The past, present, and future of martial arts are tied in with its acceptance by the public. A considerable part of that acceptance, in my opinion, is tied to the acceptance of fighting in the Olympics. For athletes of all types, the Olympics is and has been the highest level of excellence that can be achieved. Combat sports are no exception to this.

We can look at the success of boxing, wrestling, and judo for historical references. All three are among the most exciting and participated in sports in the Olympics. Wrestling is the oldest of the Olympic sports. Most recently, we have Taekwondo, and next, there will be Karate. For our purposes, let's take an examination of the latter two.

Tae Kwon Do, in my opinion, has been a very big success in the Olympics. Of course, because it is still a relatively new sport from a still young country, South Korea has won the lion's share of Olympic medals. However, it has also been very generous to places that have not won Olympic gold before. Part of this is because the World Tae Kwon Do and the Korean government has sent Tae Kwon Do emissaries out into the world to teach Tae Kwon Do.

Tae Kwon Do has bestowed medals to countries that have never had them before or have had few to remember. Tae Kwon Do came to the Olympics as a medaling event in 2000. Since that year, Jordon, Taiwan, and the Ivory Coast have won gold medals. Afghanistan, Vietnam, Niger, and Gabon also have won either silver or bronze medals in the interim. Tae Kwon Do has helped to level the playing field in sports and competition. I believe that Karate will do the same.

In my opinion, Karate was a success in the 2021 Summer Olympics. There was diversity, more than what Tae Kwon Do had. There was a wide range of medals to countries that were not considered to be the standard winners of medals, from countries that had not won Olympic medals before. However, this will change.

Eventually, there will be other martial arts in the Olympics. Who knows, something in the form of MMA, like its ancestor of Pankration, will return to the Olympics. I think that this is inevitable. I also think that this is best for the Olympics. The public is seeking a pure-blood sport that is also the ultimate athletic, mono o mono, event. MMA, as it currently is, has to be it.

Years ago, I was hooked on the idea of mixed martial arts. I loved the opening scene of

Bruce Lee's Magnus opus "Enter the Dragon." It was what our modern MMA would become. I am not the only one of a certain generation that thought this. In modern times we had Boxing, Judo, Tae Kwon Do, and now Karate. I predict; next, we will have either a resurgence of Pankration or MMA. To the victor goes the spoils!

Chapter 12: Black Belt

A question that I get all the time is, what is a black belt? The second question is how long it takes to get one. A black belt is the physical representation of a title or rank. It could just as easily be a badge, epaulet, stripes, or something else that could be shown for display.

First-degree, second-degree, or tenth-degree black belt only really means that you have been around for a long time. It does not mean that you can beat anyone who dares to step to you. The rank means something to the style but usually is meant to indicate that the wearer has reached a certain level of proficiency in that style.

"There is a difference between a martial artist and a fighter. A fighter is training for a purpose: he has a fight. I'm a martial artist. I don't train for a fight. J train for myself. J'm training all the time. My goal is perfection. But J will never reach perfection." – George St. Pierre

That person has knowledge and experience that a purple, red, or brown belt does not have. For me, the real difference between a black belt and a white belt is persistence, time, and training. The difference between a fighter and a martial artist is purpose. However, different styles do have criteria and definite processes for you to reach various levels of a black belt for their style. They are not the same even within the same art, country, or style sometimes.

For example, I have a friend who has a black belt in Goju Ryu karate. A first-degree black belt in his style should be able to do eight kata's (a set of pre-arranged forms or movements representing a fight between one or multiple opponents) plus four more that demonstrate high levels of precision and technical difficulty. He also must demonstrate 25 self-defense techniques that work against opponents attacking from the front, side, rear, while sitting, and from the ground. In addition, he must show proficiency with two weapons from the country that his martial art comes from.

A black belt, in the traditional training, no matter the style, should always be in the act of training in my eyes. A black belt is a trainer and a teacher. In certain Japanese styles, you learn all the physical techniques that you are going to learn, in some cases, by the time you are a purple belt. Later in the book, we will talk about techniques.

Having said that, the black belt is the person who has to know what they all are and when and who to teach those sorts of techniques to. It varies wildly, from style to style and country to country and organization to organization, as to what techniques should be learned, along with weapons, kata, and other things. This leads to the next question. How long should it take to get a black belt?

This is a very controversial question. Especially now and even more so in the era of mma and Jiu-jitsu. I think that it should take at least 8 to 10 years to get a black belt. In fact, I believe that there should be a universal basic requirement for a black belt and that there should be a talent test for it with a specialization patch or something identifying the style that you are in. It would be easy to do, but it will not happen because of greed, ignorance, and lack of vision. Let me explain why it will not happen first, then why it should.

Greed is the biggest factor. Without any verifiable way of knowing the real skill level of a person, they can come to a location and say that they are a black belt. They can easily say it is in a particular style that no one has ever heard of and trace their lineage to a famous instructor or master, and there is no real way to verify it. The Koreans were very smart about this. They have bodies that have the partial backing of the South Korean government, and they are in the forms of World Taekwondo and the International Taekwondo Federation.

Both bodies, specifically the World Taekwondo group, can tell you who has a black belt in their style, when they received it, who their instructor is, what they did to get the belt, and even how many people were there at the ceremony sometimes.

They receive a document that is numbered, dated, and signed by an official, the instructor and comes from Korea. In the case of the WT, it comes from the Kukkiwon. This gives the recipient the patina of legitimacy that you do not have with most styles in the USA, Europe, and in some cases, Japan.

In the USA and Europe, it should be said that there are great organizations. I have links to some of them in this book (only in the e (electronic version)), but they represent only their own styles or a select group of clubs and organizations.

A way around this would be for the federal governments in the USA, Canada, and possibly the European Union to get together and set certain standards. It's done in programming, firearms, and other endeavors and can and should be done in martial arts but specifically in karate and kung fu.

With a greater degree of standardization, there would also be a greater AND higher degree of quality. People who are interested in quality training would know exactly what they are getting and from whom. The instructors, in turn, would be able to charge a fair amount because everyone knows their pedigree and their minimum level of experience.

I look at the Gracie Brazilian Jiu-Jitsu phenomena. The Gracie family and I do not mean this as an insult because I would love to study and practice their style one day, which is a marketing juggernaut. With the advent of MMA and, specifically, the UFC (Ultimate Fighting Championship), the Gracie family has created a fighting dynasty. They have also created a way of standardization that did not exist before.

Brazilian Jiu-Jitsu, like Shotokan, Goju Ryu, Shito Ryu, and the Japanese Karate Association, before it, has the opportunity to, and from my estimation, create an organized way of setting martial arts standards that are universal. In most BJJ schools, it takes years to get a black belt. An instructor just doesn't hand it out. This was the case with many traditional styles back in the '70s and early '80s. This happened until the advent of the McDojo's.

It was whispered in the '70s and '80s but came full force in the late '80s and '90s. Schools were popping up all over the place that specifically said that you could earn a black belt in 2 years. It was prevalent in places that were marketed to younger students. This worked for hand in hand with the idea that you could learn just a few techniques with no humility, discipline, or experience fighting outside of your school or style.

I'm an old guy. By the time this book is published, I will be 60 or older. My age, to be perfectly honest, means very little. What is important is my history, knowledge, and experience with, tangentially, can be called successful and skilled martial artists and fighters. Of course, this needs a far more detailed definition than I have so far given.

We will have to do this in two parts. For this discussion, a successful fighter is someone who has been a student or athlete who has trained under someone with the expressed intent to fight completely and win X number of fights, competitions, or awards. For a boxer, it is a year to 3 years. For a martial arts fighter, it's about the same. Why? You don't have the same armature period.

For the martial artist, it is longer. In partly because of the lack of a real armature period as you have with an armature boxer. Martial artists fight within their style for long periods of time. Sometimes for two or three years. After that, they may go to open tournaments. Then to more professional venues. At this point, they have been fighting for at least four to five years. In my eyes and experience, this is about right for a young fighter.

Going back to what we were talking about initially, what is a black belt? A black belt is someone who has experience. Not just at fighting, but also at coaching, first aid, counseling, strategy, how to defend, and how to attack in both the ring and battlefield. A real black belt knows ancient weapons and modern weapons. A black belt is a master of the war arts and combat sports arts.

Chapter 13: Foundations of Success

To be successful, you must have certain qualities. All of us are imbued with these qualities naturally but have them developed at wildly different levels. Most of us do not even realize that we have them until someone recognizes them in us and points them out.

Some of us know that we have them but have no clue as to how to develop them. It does not matter what your age or gender is. History shows us that if you have these "foundational attributes," that your chances of being successful are high. These foundational attributes apply to everyone, fighter or not.

Not all these qualities will be those of the fighter. Some of them are the coach, teacher, or parent. In whatever situation, they must be at the disposal of the fighter. No individual is a complete package. This is a primary reason why the most successful people have teams developed around them to help them become successes.

It is most obvious in sports, but it is the same in other endeavors in life. Almost all successful scientists, businesspeople, entertainers, and world leaders all have teams that make them better and are the successes that we all know them to be. The following, I believe, are the attributes that you need to have or have in your team to make you an elite point fighting champion.

Desire – You must want to be a champion in order to be a champion. It has to burn at your soul. You must think of it day and night. You think of it when you first wake up and before you go to sleep at night. In my humble opinion, desire is the part of love that makes you do what you do. Desire makes you get up when you fall. Desire is the "want" in what you want. Desire is the good part of greed. It pushes you forward and keeps you going when other options falter.

Consistency – To be good at anything, you have to be consistent in doing that thing. You cannot skip workout days. You cannot forget to do drills. You absolutely have to spar. You must do these things regularly and often in order to learn and, by extension, win. Consistency is a habit that you must learn every day.

Perseverance – Perseverance is the easiest and hardest thing to learn and adapt to. You fall, you get up. You are knocked down, and you get up. You are knocked down, and the person/thing that knocked you down is still standing over you; you still get up. That person/thing that knocked you down knocks you down, again and again, you still get up. You defy the pain. You ignore the pain both physically and mentally and get up again and again. That is the essence of perseverance.

Perseverance is a numbers game. You just have to get up enough times to reach the moment when you land that blow that allows you to win. It can be on the 2nd try or the 89th try, but you will never reach it if you do not keep getting up!

The next skill sets up the start of all your core foundational qualities. These attributes are the finishing touches to desire, consistency, and perseverance. It should be noted that if you don't have them, that the members of your surrounding team must have them, as I mentioned earlier.

Communication – You, the fighter or member of the fighters' team, must be able to communicate goals, strategies, information, and most importantly, emotion and desire. It is a key attribute that all members of the fighting team know what their jobs are and what is expected of them and each other.

Fighters communicate with team members verbally, by writing, and in how they listen. Fighters sometimes hear but do not listen. You can speak to them, but they only hear what they want to hear. Team members sometimes have to communicate in nonverbal ways to the fighter. This may be via sparring or video of past fights.

On the other side of things, fighters have to listen to the people around them. They must learn to listen. Fighters are the CEOs of their teams. As such, they must learn to articulate their thoughts and ideas clearly and efficiently. This means that you, the fighter, must learn to be a good listener and learn to understand others' emotions, build strong relationships with your coaching and support team.

Initiative – To be a good fighter, you have to show initiative. It all starts with you deciding that you want to be a champion. This is a direct part of desire. You're picking and (on the professional level) hiring the right people to surround you is key to getting the ball rolling, but you have to do it. You show others your commitment and level of development by taking personal responsibility and taking proactive responsibility for things by aggressively developing your team and setting goals. You find answers or get your coaches to find them for you.

Professionalism – Professionalism is all about work ethic. To be a champion fighter, you do not have to wire a shirt and tie. You have to carry yourself in a calm, focused, and business-oriented fashion to be a next-level athlete and champion. As an example of this, I will use a mma fighter that I admire.

I am a huge fan of Fedor Emelianenko. Mr. Emelianenko was one of the greatest mma fighters ever. He is famous for his cold and business-like way of fighting. He was never emotional. It never mattered if it were a championship fight or an exhibition; he remained reserved and always about business.

Analytical – Fighters and their teams have to look at a problem and break it down into small components. From there, they methodically examine and break those into better-understood parts. Once this is done, the how's and why's of the problem can be understood, for a combat sports athlete, in the form of defenses, counters, and attacks. A good example of being analytical can be seen in football and basketball.

In both sports, there is the examination of film/video and previous analysis of the opponent that will be battled against next.

Problem solver - Challenges will arise in every job you have. You'll want to have the ability to analyze issues, make sound decisions and overcome problems. Some of this is just being persistent, but most of it is thinking analytically, methodically, and calculatingly about what the problem is. Once you can see the problem clearly, you can come up with various actions to render the issue moot.

Adaptable – No matter what, you have to be able to go with the flow. You have to be able to adjust to new challenges and opportunities. Of all people, fighters have to be adaptable and ready for change. Fighters meet new opponents; they will, without a doubt, fight, move and react differently than the last person that they have met.

Being adaptable is key to succeeding in fighting, school, business, and life. New vectors and obstacles come across all the time in our lives, the lives of our friends/loved ones, and our professional lives. Natural catastrophes, such as fires, tornadoes, hurricanes, rains, and storms of all kinds, happen, and there is nothing that we can do about them but to adapt. At these times, we can only come up with a plan to deal with what has happened. This is adaptation. Being adaptable is a defining point to being a champion fighter and second or third place.

Now let's move on to the more technical skills to success in elite point fighting.

Practice – I am going to go over this over and over again here. Hopefully, this just demonstrates how important it is. A fighter has to practice his/her craft over and over in order to learn it and, in turn, to do it. Before something can be learned to muscle memory, one has to practice a move over and over and over again. Practice, practice, drill, drill, rinse and repeat.

While doing research for this book, I found a great page by Wayne Goldsmith:

https://wgcoaching.com/sports-skills/ What is said on this page epitomizes what I think you should do as a coach and athlete when it comes to training for fighting. Check it out if you have a chance.

Commitment - This is the other side of consistency. You have to make a commitment to achieving your goals. It takes dedication and sacrifice to be a star. You have to put in the effort, time, and work to rise above the crowd of fighters out there to be a real champion. Without this, you are just another what if or could have been.

Pressure Management – This is key. If you are going to be the champ, you have to be able to handle the pressure of being on the road to be the champ, but then, after you win, you have to be able to handle the pressure of being the champ.

Luckily, it's progressive. You build up to it, and your ability to handle the pressure helps you once you arrive. Handling pressure is all part of the fight game.

Leadership - Leadership is about two things. The first and most obvious thing for a leader is being able to make a decision quickly with purpose. A leader has to be able to say yes and no to things that others either do not have the confidence or ability to do. Great leaders ask for advice because they are not scared to listen to other voices.

Second, and less known, is that leaders are visionaries. They are always thinking about the long game. Making tough decisions about the team list or the workforce; developing the ability to inspire, motivate and lead your colleagues; are skills that are always in demand.

Responsibility – This is an extension of leadership. To paraphrase an old saying, the buck stops with you. Ultimately, you can't blame other people when you are the one guiding them. When you win and are in the spotlight feeling the warmth from the crowd's adulation, you also have to be the one in the spotlight who takes the blame. Not your trainers, instructor, or coach. You. Win or lose; you have to own it.

Sportsmanship – To learn how to accept defeat is to learn how to humble yourself. When you learn how to humble yourself, you learn how to win. Winning and learning how to humble yourself starts with sportsmanship.

The role of competition is to decide on the pecking order. Combat sports have competition at its very heart. This spills over to relationships, business, and life. Life is about competition, and competition is life. We compete for everything. Sportsmanship is the foundation for how we do this.

Time Management – Both in and out of the ring, a fighter has to learn how to manage his time. The what and when happens because of how you and your team manage your time. This includes training, team meetings, business meetings, and time with doctors.

Branding – Branding is key to your long-term success as a fighter. It's not about your nickname or what people like to call you, but it is about what they think about you. It is the reputation that will act as your calling card. When thinking about your brand, you will have to think about what you are fighting for. Your image/reputation should be what your professional/business visages. This has to be a well-thought-out strategy.

By now, it should be clear that you will have two images that you will have to juggle simultaneously, the fighter in the ring and the businessperson. One is a beast, and the other is about finance. As you get older and fight less, the businessperson persona will become more important than the former. What is at stake will be how many fights and opportunities to fight bigger named combatants and potential endorsements.

Legacy - A sign of success, as I see it, is what you leave behind to say that you lived a good life and contributed to the betterment of society. When people look back on your life after you are gone, what will they think about you? What good deeds will you be remembered for? What do you do with the money and fame that come with being a champion-level elite fighter?

This is where your team comes into play or the part of your team that you don't see every day. Every fight team has (for combat sports) a boxing coach, grappling coach, kicking coach, strength and conditioning coach, and a head coach. However, the super-elite fighters have a lawyer and an accountant that are central to their success too.

They help navigate you through the maze of groupies (yes, point fighting has groupies), the sudden flush of money (this comes if you go pro), and constant tug for your attention when you "arrive" as a champion. They help with purchases of big-ticket items, and most importantly,

making your money makes you more money. They also help you from hurting yourself financially.

Nothing is worse than being a champ today, and five years afterward, you are broke and have nothing to show for all of your hard work and victories.

Your lawyer and account are often overlooked but are an essential part of your team and long-term success. Together they help you keep, hold and manage your money. At the beginning of your fighting career, the person that is your fighting instructor/coach is more important to your success. Towards the middle and later parts, it will be your lawyer and account.

For example, your lawyer (sometimes) acts as your legal advisor and as an agent. They have what is called a fiduciary responsibility to serve your needs in legal and financial areas. They negotiate your deals and contracts towards your benefit and best interest.

Your lawyer is always on the lookout for new and better fights like you, and your coach will too. They also do the research to ensure that the people you are doing business with are on the up and up. The next member of your team is your accountant.

The accountant makes sure that your money is where it is going to make you the most money and keeps tabs on where your money has been, is at, and will be. Let me explain that last part clearer. Your account follows your money. They check to see if the money that you have in your account is coming from some shady cartel in Eastern Europe trying to launder their cash. They make sure that the bank(s) that you put your money in is a solid and fiscally stable institution.

They also make sure that you have full and secure access to your money. What good is having it if you cannot access it when and where you want. Finally, accountants make sure that your money makes you money.

Your accountant and lawyer make sure that you have strong legitimate investments that give you the most ROI (return on investment). They help you buy money-making businesses instead of losing money on fancy cars and fur underwear (I'm looking at your Mike Tyson.)

They also keep you from shooting yourself in the foot because they keep you from purchasing things that lose money.

Your legacy will be the truest and only indicator of whatever success you have managed to have in life.

Your legacy will be an indication as to how

faithful you have been to the foundations of success that we have laid out here. This is not hyperbole. This is life. Live your life as if each day will be your last and as if you are carving your name on the stones of time!

Chapter 14: Fighting Spirit

Fighting spirit is simple to explain. You know what it is just by saying the words. For those that are a little younger and possibly less aware, let me explain it. It is all about what is inside of the fighter. What motivates them to fight and, more importantly, what pushes them forward to fight.

It is about that spark. That speaks to the fighter to fight. It is what makes a fighter a fighter. It is the spark that exist in every fighter. Of course, we come to the question of "what is a fighting spirit?"

Fighting spirit is not a simple thing to define or explain. It is not a philosophy, but it does have a philosophical part to it. It is an ability. It is a skill. It is a superpower. It is a fighter shield against fear.

When in battle, self-defense, and even in competition, the smell of fear is always there. It permeates everything. No one wants to die or feel pain. Both of these things cause fear. Fear also comes from, in the realm of competitive fighting, the thought of possibly losing.

It is just in human nature to want to win. The thought of not winning is the start of fear. It is that kernel of thought that is the fertile ground from which it takes root and grows. The idea of losing is like a slap across the face. Fear, or at least the idea of it, is always at the edge of your thoughts. It may not be obvious at first, but it is there.

When you are using your fighting spirit, you are doing your best, but you are doing it with conviction and bravery. Fighting spirit does not mean that you have conquered fear. However, it does mean that you are not allowing fear to hold you back. I, as a person who seeks to do brave things, know what fear is. I am afraid of heights, yet I jump out of airplanes.

I was a combat medic in the Army. I never knew when I would be forced into battle. When I did, when I was faced with a struggle and the sword of death was there to strike me down, my supper power of fighting spirit was my shield.

I am afraid of my wife, yet I still do whatever it is that I do. Of course, I don't remember it after she knocks me out, but I stand there and do it again. This is fighting spirit. (Actually, in my case, it's just a lack of grey matter and common sense, but you get my meaning.) Of course, you have to wonder, can I develop a fighting spirit, and the answer is yes, you can.

As it is with all important things, you have to start small and build up to it. Most people cannot conquer a mountain in a day. Some can, but most of us cannot. You start off with a slight incline and build your way up to a mountain. In competitive fighting, that means you start fighting your coach or instructor, and they, in turn, will perform a little test.

The little test that you will start with is with your instructor or coach testing your defenses. They will test how you react to small things. A jab here and a kick there. A kick here and a back fist there.

They will build up their attacks then stop. Next, they will put in either another instructor or beginner sparring partner. They will observe your reactions and see if it matches up with what they saw with you when you sparred them. Lastly, they'll bring the pain.

This last part is necessary but painful. Your coach or instructor has to find out what you are either afraid of or where you are weak at. This is important because they can't correct your weakness or discover what you fear without it. This is where they turn you into a superhero.

You are becoming an elite fighter and a superhero, and it starts here. Or better phrased, this is where you begin to see all of your training start to take shape. Some people start to see it quickly. Others it takes time.

Whatever way that it takes you, it doesn't matter. What does matter is that your instructor and your teammates see it. Change is happening. They can see the sparks of your fighting spirit start to develop and grow. This is when and where you become a champion and develop your Spidey sense. No radioactive spider needed.

Chapter 15: Fight Team

No matter what style you have and no matter what your goals are, you must surround yourself with the people who are going to support you and help you achieve your goals. I've talked about this before, but it bears repeating. Let us start with the key person, outside of the fighter, of course, the coach.

For most people in martial arts, their coach is their instructor, or at least it is in the very beginning. This is a natural and very common setup. However, as one grows as an athlete, one needs the talents of a coach. This begs the question, what does a coach do?

A coach of any kind has to wear various hats. They also must understand different skill sets.

This is true if the coach works with individuals or teams. The major areas that they have to be knowledgeable in are exercises for improving basic technical skills. This is done by the coach analyzing the current level of skills that the athlete has and comparing that to the athletes that they will compete against. Once that comparison is made, the coach will develop the balance of exercises and drills needed for the athlete to compete and win.

Most coaches like to utilize exercises, conditioning, drills, and a sparring regimen that meet the needs of their fighters. This may or may not frequently change depending on the fighter and the philosophy of the coach. What the coach does and recommends will extend into realms outside of the gym. Coaches will, until a specialist is interviewed and assigned to do it, will advise the athlete on how to eat and sleep.

I should point out that most advanced fighters, point, and mma, have specialty coaches. In the beginning, most people only have one coach. As I said earlier, they will wear multiple hats. This will go on until the fighter is a serious competitor.

For a point fighter, this means that you compete nationally at major tournaments and are ready to or are receiving endorsements. The same for mma, but the measurement is breaking into the top 50 in your division or weight class. In either case, your coach is now your head coach, and you have specialist coaches that report to him.

For the point fighter, the specialty coaches are strength and conditioning coaches and possibly a nutritionist. For the mma fighter, it is the same, with kicking, striking, and grappling (i.e., wrestling, judo, Brazilian Jiu-jitsu, sambo) coaches. All of these other coaches are assistants to the main coach. In fact, I highly recommend that the fighter and head coach interview each of the other coaches together.

There are two types of head coaches for fighters. The first type is a mentor and guide. This type of coach is ideal for the fighter who wants to get from a to b and is looking for someone to take them there. The fighter who likes this type of coach is the same as who would like to have a self-driving car.

The second type is an advisor. This type of coach gives information and data to the fighter, and they decide on the direction that they want to go in. This fighter likes to drive the car themselves. Both types of coaches are successful, but ultimately it is the fighter who must decide on what they are comfortable with.

Assistant coaches do not report to the fighter but the head coach. The reason for this is that the fighter must learn to listen to one voice for guidance and not 4 or 5. They have to keep their heads clear and stay focused. The head coach has taken all the information and advice from the assistant coaches and THEN sits down with the fighter.

Often assistant coaches are trying to develop their skills to be head coaches. I highly recommend those that read this book and are interested in becoming coaches to go to a dojo or gym and speak to a few people that you admire and get tips from them.

Being a coach is like being a marriage counselor, prison warden, mother, father, and drill sergeant all in one. As for the actual technical part of the job, there are only a few things you need to do. Let us take the kicking coach as an example.

The first thing that a kicking coach has to do, and this is the same with any of the coaches (head or assistant), is find out where your fighter is right when you meet them. Where were they physically when you met them? What type of shape are they in? How strong are they? What is their weight? Should they lose or gain weight? How flexible are they? What sort of stamina and endurance do they have? Do they have accurate kicks? Are they offensive or defensive fighters? How do they kick when they are tired or injured? What are their favorite kicks, and why? These are only a few of the questions that a fighter's coach

has to ask but are the foundation to everything
that they will help the fighter become a champion
eventually.

Training

Training has several major components and a few
minor ones. We start with, and this is very specific
to this book and its topic, traditional training, and
modern training. The components for both
involve diet, exercise, and conditioning (with the
last two having sub-topic areas of interest for
fighters, trainers, and teachers). Let us start with
the difference between traditional training and
modern. What they are, who they are for and when
to use them.

Before we go on, let me talk about the two
things I get asked about a lot which are exercise
and conditioning. What are they? What do they do

for me? These are always major questions and the first things that I answer and talk about.

Exercise is for developing strength and power, and conditioning is for endurance and stamina. No matter what your goal is, exercise and conditioning must be part of making you the best version of who you are as a fighter.

Traditional training is made for someone who is in the martial arts to be an instructor of that art and would like to keep the ideas, history, and philosophy of their art alive. One ingredient is to learn how the ancestors of the art trained and why they trained a certain way. It is fervently believed, by some, that if they train the way that the greats of their style did, that they will in turn harvest the skills and strengths that they had.

There is some legitimacy to this argument. For karate and kung fu artist, there is a certain pride that is expressed when students can say that they are doing a particular exercise exactly the way that a grandmaster did over a hundred or hundreds of years ago. There is also the fact that their style has survived after generations of students, teachers, and fighters who trained the same way, and the style still exists.

Now just as it was in ancient times, fighters have certain goals that they want to attain. It doesn't matter if a person is a warrior or combat athlete; the aim of the training is the same. How do I get stronger, faster, and tougher? Fighters want to make their bodies in shape so that they can take what their opponents are dishing out. They want their hands and feet hard so that when they connect that it hurts or breaks something.

There is no doubt in my mind that is what our martial forefathers thought when I look at some of their training methods. Let us start by looking at how they trained their hands.

From what I have been able to garner from my studies, in particular Japan and China, exercises to toughen all parts of the hand were incredibly important. It took years for them to get the striking areas of the hand to become the weapons that they are famed for. Special attention was given to the tips of the fingers, the first two knuckles from the thumbs, edge of the inner and outer parts of the hand. Similarly, attention was given to the foot. The ball, heel, instep (up to the same

You and I (more than likely you do not realize it yet) live in an amazing time of change. At least in the martial arts. Every twenty to thirty years, we go through a breathtaking period of innovation and change at a fundamental level. Usually, the public is totally unaware of the breakneck speed at which things change, but for those that are, it is revolutionary. This is happening in the martial arts, and we are right in the middle of a major change.

I have been through this before. For me, the first time was in the 1970s. I did not grasp it at the time, but the martial artist was in the middle of a revolution, and it began with a guy named Bruce Lee. He changed martial arts in a lot of ways but in one of the most dramatic ways was in the way that we train.

For centuries martial artists in Japan, Korea, China, and all over the south and southeast of Asia fighters trained in a particular way. When many of the styles that we currently practice in the West (Jiu-Jitsu, Iaido, Hwarang, Kung Fu, et al.) were originally developed, they were meant for combat on the battlefield. The regular foot soldier was conscripted and had to be trained and ready to fight in a very short period of time. The training that they were given was often brutal and repetitive.

It also had to be simple and to the point, much like what basic training is for modern-day soldiers. The areas of concern for ancient leaders and trainers of soldiers would be if they were physically fit to fight, did they know how to use various weapons that were popular in their era, i.e., spears, swords, and knives. As time went on, these fighting skills transitioned from martial ways and into martial arts.

This is an important thing to understand so that I will go into a little detail. For the modern student, enthusiast, teacher, coach, and scholar, fighting has three pillars, and they are the martial way (military combat skills), martial arts (karate, taekwondo, kung fu), and combat sports (MMA, Thai Boxing, Kendo/Gumdo). Each one has a different purpose and serves a different audience.

Martial ways are only interested in the most effective and easily learned fighting method. The fighting methods that they are interested in are dynamic hand-to-hand interactions that inflict death and can be used to control an enemy force.

Martial arts are, for the great majority, aimed at civilians. There is a large self-defense component to it. Historical weapons are learned and practiced. There is also an intellectual element along with a philosophical component in the fighting. The goal is like what it is for someone going to university. The process of attending makes the student a better person physically, morally, and intellectually.

Combat sport participants are looking for techniques that are not deadly but have a visual and physical impact. Combat sports participants are not trying to kill or maim opponents. There are no attacks on the throat, eyes, or knees. This is a competition, and the aim is to entertain.

Competitors gain points by striking certain areas of the body, takedowns, and in some cases gaining submissions. All three of these areas of interest have various methods of training.

Before we go into the next topic, let us not be remiss and forget to discuss injuries. This is one of the areas that there is always going to be lots of debate about. Should you train when injured or not. As it is with a lot of things, it depends. It depends on where the injury is, the type of injury, and of course, the severity of the injury.

Of course, for most fighters, the important thing is that the injury makes you look like a wussy. Right after that is, will you look like a wussy if you don't work out while injured. Let us put these to the side and talk about what you need to do before you even tackle these topics. The first thing you must do is see your doctor.

Nothing, absolutely nothing matters until you see and hear from your doctor. This is one of the few times I will advise you to skip what your coach and teammates may tell you. Your doctor will make sure that your injury is not life-threatening. They will ensure that you are able to continue to fight and do so to the best of your physical ability. You will get CAT scans, MRI's and X-rays that will look at every inch of your muscle, bone, and soft tissue.

I would highly recommend that, if you can, get and keep copies of your medical and dental records. Put them on a flash drive or store them in the cloud but have quick access to them. The fighter and coach should be able to provide a new doctor with X-rays of past injuries and issues of concern.

This is especially important if you get hurt out of state or out of the country. Having this information allows doctors and healthcare agents the ability to provide you with the best care possible and make decisions that will keep you alive and healthy. Either carry a copy of the pertinent information with you or have access to it.

Equipment Check Sheet

At the bare minimum, we are all born with all of the equipment that we need to train. We have arms, hands, legs, and feet that we use to punch, kick and throw with. Most importantly, we have heads. On that head, we have eyes to see with, ears to hear, and a brain to decipher all of the information that they present to our brains. We are born with the ability to think. The ability to think is undervalued and underappreciated. Even with these amazing bodies and brains that we have, there are a few things that we can and should have that will make us better.

There is a whole range of equipment that a
fighter/combat athlete can and should use. I will
list what I think are the bare basics and identify if
it is for a traditional or modern fighter. Before we
get to that, it should be pointed out that you might
be in one group and see an exercise or piece of
equipment in another category and say to yourself
that you want to try that. By all means, PLEASE
do so! This is exactly how innovation and
improvement start. In fact, I encourage you to
experiment with everything that you see and read
here.

Basic Traditional Equipment

Traditional martial artists are human. When
something has proven itself to work and can easily
be accessed by practitioners, they use it. Tradition
will always take a backseat to what works for most.

However, there are things that remain that are must-haves in the training repertoire. I personally have used, at one time or another, all of the equipment that I write about here, but I should point out that some of these items are rare, even in the most traditional of gyms. The first thing that comes to mind is the makiwara or punching board.

The makiwara will probably never be used by mma fighters. Most consider it a relic of the past and ineffective. However, for the real traditionalist who has the goal of strengthening their wrist, hands, and knuckles, the makiwara is hard to beat. You can tell someone who used it because their knuckles are enormous.

The strikes trained on the makiwara are reverse punch, ridge hand, knife hand, elbow strike, and back fist. The use of the makiwara toughens and strengthens the contact areas used for striking better than a bag by far. It also helps to develop power in your techniques. Next is the heavy club.

The heavy club is another strengthening tool. It looks like a long baseball bat. Maybe 5-6 feet long and 10 to 20 pounds. It can be made out of wood or metal. You swing it from either side and stop it right in front of you. You will need space to use it.

You will also swing it in a chopping motion from the top of your head, bringing it down to the level of your navel. In both cases, you want to stop the motion of the club abruptly. This will help in developing back and shoulder strength. Our next item is called the iron geta (clogs).

The clogs are nothing more than footwear made of iron. In the USA, Europe, Africa, and South America, you will be hard-pressed, I would imagine, to find traditional wooden getas (conventional Japanese footwear), let alone iron ones. An easy substitution would be leg or ankle weights.

I would only use these under supervision and with great care. I have seen younger and novice students hyperextend their knees while using the getas and ankle weights. Next is the body stretcher box.

I have only seen the body stretcher in a few schools. The box is the length of a person's body and about three feet wide. The box is roughly ten inches deep. Right at the top and across the center is a sit that is three feet across and inches wide

long

Equipment:

Equipment	Traditional	Point	MMA	Muay Thai	TKD	Athlete
Vinyl Chest Guard						
Vinyl kick						
Vinyl punch						
Vinyl shin						
Mouthguard						
Carry bag						
Cloth fist protector						
Cloth shin protector						
Cloth shin/ instep protector						
Cloth backfist/knuckle protector						
Heavy bag						
Grappling dummy						

Hand wraps						
Boxing gloves						
Vinyl headgear						
Female Chest Protector						
Vinyl rib protector						
Makiwara						
Vinyl Chest Guard						

Chapter 16 – Coaches and Trainers and What to Do

Next to being a fighter, the hardest job in the sport is coaching the fighter. It calls for a lot of time and dedication. The role of the coaches and trainers of the fighter is to get them physically and psychologically prepared for battle. In most fighters' lives, the coach and trainers are all one person. As the fighter becomes more successful, they can and usually will bring on talent that can help in very specific areas.

If you can get other people to come on board, the people that you will need will be part of your team for a few years at least. We will talk about this multiple times in this book and with various levels of detail. Let's start off with the head coach.

The head coach will more than likely be your head instructor at your gym, school, or dojo. This is usually a good thing because they know who you are and should have a great idea of what you can do. By the time you are ready to fight on a bigger stage, they would have been with you for 2 to 3 years.

Your head coach will be responsible for scheduling your workouts and examining your progress. They will also advise the fighter on how to grow as a fighter. If there is a hole in your game, your coach will and should be the first person to fix it.

As you progress in fighting, the coach will assist the fighter in making that move. Until you are ready to move on to more heavy contact fights, a general head coach will do. However, once you start to think about moving up to the big leagues, you must bring on other trainers. First on your list should be a strength and conditioning coach.

Your strength and conditioning coach (scc) job is to make sure that you are at your physical best when it's time to fight. In conjunction with your head coach, they pick the training protocols that you will adopt along with the exact exercises that you will perform. They will make sure that along every rung of the ladder to your fight, that you are exactly where you should be in power and ability.

If you decide that you want to go the mma route, you will also need striking and grappling coaches. However, I would highly recommend that even if you do not take that path, and there is nothing wrong with that, I would suggest that you find these people and work out with them. Even if you go to a Kickboxing/Boxing/Muay Thai (take your pick) gym and then do a wrestling or Jiu-Jitsu academy once or twice a month, that would be okay. Why? Because as a martial artist, you want to be as well round as possible. My kicking boxing coach made me take wrestling in high school, and I am forever grateful to him for that. I became a more complete fighter because of it.

The coaches and trainers must both be trusted and absolutely ruthless in what and how they do their jobs. Their assessments and recommendations have long-reaching impacts on the success of the fighter. They are the people who are responsible for not just giving positive feedback and tips on techniques but providing wisdom on what to do once the fighter has achieved success. However, like the fighter, the coaches need help too!

Coaches should take advantage of classes on how to teach. A fighting coach is a teacher, mother, father, psychologist, and a nanny. Being a good coach is all about learning and observing. Anyone can look at a fight, but can you break the fight down into its component parts. I would recommend classes at community college or pursuing a more advanced degree. Kinesiology, nutrition, physiology, sports science, physical education, psychology are all degrees or classes that would be perfect for would-be coaches.

Point fighting coaching has two phases to it. One is the pre-fight, and the other is the fight day. The pre-fight is all about the preparation for the day of the fight. The big elements are the training and setting of goals. The second one is the day of the fight. That has two parts to it. We start with the before hitting the mat/ring and into what happens when you are in front of your opponent. Let us start with the pre-phase.

We begin with the planning stage. The questions that we need answers to are why, what, and how. The why part is easy; our fighter would like to win and become an elite fighter. They have set a goal of winning 4 top tournaments in the upcoming year. The what is also easy.

We set a very clear and concise training regimen of exercises, drills, and sparring schedule to achieve the goals that the coaches and fighters believe will help attain their dream. Once a week, the coaches, trainers, and fighters sit down to go over goals and to see where they are in the timeline to achieve success.

How? We will train x times a day a week with light sparring three times a week and heavy twice a week. We will also go to compete at smaller venues to access progress. In addition to this, we will also go and watch x number of fights at x number of smaller tournaments to scout competition and check for trends, and to put together dossiers on judges. Active competitors must know the judges and referees so that they can understand how they think and what they like. It happens in all combat sports but is especially true in the point tournament arena.

Something that is not often talked about, and when it is, not enough. The psychological aspects of being a coach. The coach is a father, mother, best friend, teacher, boy/girlfriend, priest, imam, rabbi, and shrink all rolled into one. The coach is the one that they will tell that they are not good enough to fight. The coach has to be the one who assures them that they can do this.

During the first and second phases of the fight, the coach must be Tony Robbins and be the ultimate motivator. Coach "I'm not ready!" Coach "It's 2 am in the morning, and I fight at 10 am. What do I do?" Coach "I can't beat any of those guys!!!" On and on, the coach is going to hear this sort of thing and has to be ready for it. This is going to happen all through the training phase and on the fight day.

Critical to the job of the coach is to make sure that you do not peak before a major tournament. You can have a fighter go to a few small tournaments before the big day, but just to get a feel for how the fighter is physically and psychologically. If you go this route, make sure that it's at least a month out from the primary fight that you are training for.

Additionally, when you do this, make sure that you have a video of their fighting. It is crucial that you have two or three cameras so that you can film each fight and review it afterward. In fact, I would highly recommend it for your training sessions.

The cameras must be set up at at least three angles. Camera one is behind the fighter showing his viewpoint. Camera two is from behind the opponent, and three is from the judge's area. If you have your own gym or dojo, hang a camera from the ceiling also. If you can get headgear with a go-pro built into it, I would use it on one for the sparring partner and the other for the fighter.

This is super helpful for the coach because when you have video from various angles AND visual data from the viewpoint of the sparring partner and the fighter. Decisions on how to move, how to change patterns, and most importantly, if the fighter is telegraphing their movements. All of this is about being ready, physically relaxed, and psychologically prepared.

The second phase is fight day. Here we have several small components that have to really be looked at. The first is the pre-fight setup. The very first thing that a coach, not a trainer, has to do is scout out a place where his fighter and crew can be as alone as possible. This is going to be the "fighters bubble." This will happen even if they decide to go professional. The bubble is just a spot where the fighter can be alone with one or two other people and relax and get physically and mentally ready to rumble.

In the bubble, you will assuage the fighter's fears. Make sure you know where a bathroom is. I used to have to take a dump just before I fought. It didn't matter if it was a big tournament or small. I always had to use the bathroom. Some people have to throw up. It is just nerves, and they ofttimes manifest themselves physically.

In the early days and with smaller tournaments, the coach, crew, and friends are going to be out on the floor glad-handing and doing the whole meet and greet with the judges, referees, and audience members that are there. The goal is to talk up your fighter. You are developing a mythology around them.

This is where you start to tell their story. Your fighter gains power by people knowing who they are. Talk about the fights that they have had in an ad which they have beat and how amazing they are. You are creating a story that others can tell, which helps to promote your fighter. While this is happening, your fighter is relaxing and getting ready to go on "stage."

Someone has to stay with the fighter at all times. This person has only one job, and that is to keep the fighter by their selves and focusing on what is to happen later. The fighter should be doing very light drills, stretching, and warming up. This should consist of light target drills, pushups, jumping jacks, sit-ups, stance switches, and a light massage maybe. The goal is to have a light sweat going about 10 to 20 minutes before hitting the mats. All this should happen within the "fight bubble."

While walking towards and to the fight area, the coach should be next to or behind the fighter. No pointers are talked about, only motivation and settling of nerves. Nothing else is happening at this point. Once at the mat, the coach should start to set the team-up. This should be discussed before you even get to the tournament. Everyone should know exactly where they should be and what they should be doing.

The coach should acknowledge or at least say hello to the judges and center referee. Your entire team should be cordial and friendly; however, the only people that the judges and referees should know are the fighter and the coach. In point tournaments, at least in most places, coaches are not allowed to talk as the fight is going on. This means that as soon as the fighters step out on the mat, they want to be able to speak until the fight is over.

Now, if you are lucky enough to be at a tournament where you can talk while the fight is going on, you should have some phrases ready for your fighter. Some people go the way of football players and will have numbers and certain "plays" practiced. I'm not too sure of this. I personally only know of two coaches that have utilized this type of strategy, and their success has been spotty. I am a fan of the traditional boxing strategy by keeping calls simple. Let me give you a few examples.

Remember, point fighting is very fast and has lots of blitzing going on all of the time, much to my chagrin. This gives you little room to convey anything to your fighter. This means that any orders or advice you want while still fighting must be short and to the point.

For example, you can yell out: 1. "jam and counter," 2."hit angles," 3."spin center," 4."ax on retreat," and 5"attack" (1. Check kick and come back with a roundhouse. 2. Come off the center line and kick or punch. 3. Use a spinning kick to the midsection of the opponent. 4. Use an ax kick as soon as you move backward after an attack. 5. Be aggressive and jam the fighter up.)

Most point tournaments do not have breaks between rounds if they have multiple rounds at all. If they do, this is when they will give advice and suggestions. If they do not, the coach has to make sure that the fighter is only listening to them and no one else if the tournament allows for speaking to the fighter while the fight is going on. Yes, family, friends, and others will be there, but the only voice that the fighter should hear and listen to is their coach until the fight is over.

Being a coach is hard, but it can be enjoyable and rewarding. Like a teacher, when your student wins, you feel great because you were part of their success. It is very close to being a parent. When your kid does something great and overcomes those pitfalls of life and those who thought they could defeat them, it makes you feel great! Some of the light that shines on them shines on you, and that can be a wonderful thing.

Chapter 17 – Training: Modern and Traditional Ideas about Training

Modern and traditional ideas of fighting change every five to ten years. Those changes, in my opinion, can be subtle and very nuanced. However, there are certain core ideals that stay the same. This chapter is dedicated to, what I consider, those core differences. Let me outline what the differences are between the ideas of a modern and traditional train.

Modern martial arts training is sometimes thought of reality-based fighting. No nonsense and straight to the point competition and combat is the goal for people who fall under this rubric. The same goes for

I think of myself, and I think that there is little doubt of this, that I am a modern martial artist. I believe that it is essential that we all practice grappling, particularly modern grappling in the form of Jiu-jitsu, Judo, and or wrestling. Why? You need to know how to take an opponent to the ground and what to do when you get to the ground.

I think that weight training must be part of the serious martial artist and fighter's regimen of training. All these small components are part of the arsenal of the modern and traditional fighters' repertoire. Let me first explain the difference between the two.

Modern martial arts look at and see's fighting as being a very practical thing. For the modern fighter, if it doesn't work, don't use it. They want efficient and practical tools to defeat their opponents. This makes perfect sense in their eyes. As I am sure that it is obvious to you, this is the core philosophy of mixed martial artists.

Traditionalists look at fighting slightly differently. The traditionalist is those that are worried about self-defense. How will their students prepare for it, and how they prepare and train those that come after them to train the next group of others that want to defend themselves. Central to all of it is self-defense.

For a traditionalist, nothing is more important than combat and self-defense. This way of looking at things is essential to martial arts. For the last four decades in magazines like Black Belt, Kung Fu Illustrated, Karate Illustrated, and Combat, the core discussion has been around realistic fighting. To be honest, all of these magazines were started under the premise of presenting what is accurate and most effective. Of course, isn't this the wish of every martial artist?

A mixed martial artist is no different.

The difference is that their goals are more athletic and dynamic. What techniques are central to most modern, i.e., mixed martial artists? This is going to be the stance. Why? It is the launchpad for all techniques.

When we think about the stance, the most modern martial artist often uses the boxer's wide stance. Gone is the side-to-side stance of the traditional karate and taekwondo fighters. The wider stance is the launchpad for, what they view, a better selection of weapons.

With this boxer's stance, the jab is more fluid and accurate. They can move into hooks and angled attacks and retreats more efficiently than they could in the side-to-side horse stance that is only front and back.

Hooked punches are more powerful due to the wider stance. The stance allows for a better rotation of hips and back which leads to increased power. Now a fighter can launch a close-in hook or a long-range haymaker style punch. Both can easily be turned into a counter elbow attack, rear power punch, or a fancy spinning backfist. All this from a wider stance.

A wider stance also allows a mma fighter to deliver stronger kicks to the legs and lower torso. The wider stance requires that the fighter have better control and torque from the hips.

Of course, traditional fighters are not athletes. Their goal is not to hear the throng of the crowd. They have no desire to score a knockout or win a bonus for the most spectacular technique of the night. For the traditionalist, the only thing that is important is that they live to see the next day, and they will do whatever is necessary to do that. Unlike the mma fighter, where you only have one type of person (yes, this is a blanket statement and an overgeneralization, but it suits our purpose for this chapter), the traditionalist is split in two.

On one side, you have the traditionalist who desires to be an instructor (i.e., sifu, sabunim, or sensei). This is the person who learns all aspects of fighting. They know the historical reasons for a technique and its context, they can explain the reason and theory why a technique is done, and most importantly, teach how a technique would be used for a particular person.

A traditional instructor wears multiple hats. They are a coach, academics, theoretician, advisor, and teachers. Few people can do this. It takes decades to master it and become someone who can do all these things. On the other side of the coin is the person who can teach the physical technique, how to do it, and possibly when to do it. There is nothing wrong with this because this is what most students want. In fact, at least in recent history, the ranking systems in Japanese, Korean, Vietnamese, and how Thai and Chinese styles are viewed comport to this idea.

A good instructor is one who can make a fighter better. This is the same as what a decent coach does. A decent coach shows a fighter various techniques, how and when to use them. They also learn what motivates that particular fighter. However, a good instructor goes further.

A good instructor teaches what, how, and why along with historical perspectives along with examples that are analogous to what they are going through. A good traditional instructor also teaches people who go on to be good coaches and people who want to be better instructors. A traditional instructor should be someone who knows how not just to teach the fighter but also the other coaches that the fighter surrounds himself with.

Modern fighting, here I mean in general boxing/grappling, but in particular, MMA is less concerned about history than a traditional instructor would be. Neither are they as tied to tradition. What is important, and I do agree with this, is if the person can fight. As we all know, if we have been around for a while, every that says that they can fight can throw down.

It started, in the modern era, with Bruce Lee. Or at least it did in the ether of the public's perception of the idea. An effective technique in the "real world" is what is important. Who else thinks this? The military.

I am saying that we harken to the idea of martial (war/military) arts. We fight and use techniques to defeat our opponent/enemy. To do this, we train with what we know works, and that can be taught to the widest range of people. We want the greatest results with the most minimal of training. Here is where we have a difference.

The traditionalist teaches all techniques and, in every variation, along with every scenario that it has already been used in. The modernist uses only techniques that are shown to be effective in the most common of uses. It is a longer and harder road for the traditionalist. This is the reason why it takes so long to be a good teacher.

On the other hand, it is still hard to be a modern coach or instructor. In this case, you must be ready to show it. Modern instructors are younger, more aggressive, and probably have been either fighters or, like in boxing, big fans of fighting already. Like the traditionalist, they are students, likely, of the craft of fighting.

In the long run, modern and traditionalist vision and training merge, or at least with does with the everyday folk who utilize it. The ones who have their noses in the dirt. Those that are working the grindstone day in and day out. These folks see eye to eye. The art at its most beautiful is a work of violent beauty and the training of it must go on.

Chapter 18 - Medic: Injuries and Healing

Fighters get hurt all the time. Point fighters, boxers, mma fighters, kickboxers, judoka, karateka, wrestlers, and everyone in between gets hurt from time to time. I used to tell my students that if they make it to black belt, they will probably have broken or fractured at least one or two bones.

If they make it to a 3rd-degree black belt, add on a concussion, a torn muscle, and maybe another broken bone to the mix. This is assuming that you are only doing things part-time and just doing kata, self-defense, and sparring a few times a year at a bare minimum. If you are doing more, which I have, triple the injuries.

Everything from cauliflower ear to boxers' nose and broken bones happens when it comes to people hitting, grabbing, submitting, kicking, punching, and other unpleasant things. This means that all black belts and some schools make this a requirement for their black belt test, take cpr and first aid classes to get promoted.

I agree with this as a requirement for any advanced martial arts practitioner. If you are a severe fighter (and you are a serious fighter if you train 4 – 7 days a week and have done so for more than a year), you hope to be an instructor or coach; you must learn cpr and basic first aid.

For those of you who are promoters, coaches, or gym owners, I would highly recommend that you find a doctor/medic, physical therapist, and a masseuse that you can call or bring on board. The doctor is for before the fighter starts training hard for a new fight. You also need them for check-ups after a big tournament or fight. The medic is for everything in between. You should have a medic at the gym and have them go to fights with you.

Medics are used for emergency injuries and are easier to find. Medics will help you immensely when injuries happen and help in creating a rehabilitation game plan for most injuries. In the meantime, you should start learning a few things on your own.

Next up are the physical therapist (pt) and masseuse. The pt is there to make sure body function and mobility are where they should be at. You should probably have your fighter have a visit every two to three weeks. The pt will work hand

and hand with your medic or one of your trainers, if not the head coach. Check them out a few times a week after a training or fight injury.

I would highly recommend that you ask your pt about getting a masseuse. In many cases, they either have them working at the same place that they work out of or work directly with them with some of their other customers. A good masseuse will learn your body over time. Really good ones can be invaluable when it comes to your rehabilitation and future training.

You do not have to know how to do field surgery, but you should know how to set a splint, apply a pressure bandage, what to do in case of a concussion, and stop bleeding from a cut or minor wound. These are essential things because in training and at tournaments, you will eventually see these sorts of things, and someone must take care of them when they do. That someone is you!

I am not a doctor, which means I cannot tell you the whys and hows of the injuries that you will eventually come across; what I can do is tell you about the most common ones and where you will see them at. Let's start with the ones common to the workout area.

Most of your workout injuries are due to stress or push/pull action. The stress can be from lifting too much weight or poor body mechanics when lifting. The stress can come from simple light weights or even bodyweight with poor alignment or mechanics when performing the lift.

Bad body alignment is the usual culprit when it comes to lower back injuries, which come from stress to both the joints and muscles of the back.

The biggest culprits are deadlifts and squats. I highly recommend that when performing either exercise that you do it with a trainer or partner present each time.

When practicing either of these, body alignment is key to you not hurting yourself. Alignment and the proper mechanics when performing the deadlift are key to you not suffering long-term or debilitating injury. Always start off with the lightest weight possible and practice alignment and proper mechanics until both you and your coach are confident that you understand what you are supposed to do. In a later chapter, I will go over the mechanics of what to do and how to perform the action.

The bench press is similar in several stress issues caused by lifting. The bones and muscles of the shoulders, chest, elbows, and wrist receive the greatest amount of stress. Pushups can also cause stress to these areas but with less severity.

In both cases, the best way to minimize stress fractures is to perform the motions correctly. The standard push-up is the easiest one to correct. Later in the book, we will have links to web pages that demonstrate what I consider the best way to perform these actions.

Another huge area of stress is on the ankles and knees. If you go to a lot of tournaments or kickboxing matches, you will see former fighters in their 60's or 70's walking around.

You will notice that a lot of them limp. In fact, you will see this with athletes from other contact sports. Just look at former military people and athletes involved in soccer, American football, basketball, and other sports where the legs were a key component of how they performed.

The most damaging leg issue is an anterior cruciate ligament or ACL tear. A torn ACL is just an awful injury to have because it can have life-changing impacts on your athletic and personal life. Those fighters with the limp that I mentioned in the previous paragraph have probably been victims of torn ACLs. The good thing is that surgery and rehabilitation usually help with getting you back on course. The best thing, however, is to try and prevent an ACL tear from ever happening. This is done by exercising properly.

The most common injury for the knee is a knee sprain. This is reasonably easy to take care of. Like so many things, there is an acronym for how to deal with it. It is called R.I.C.E. (rest, ice, compression, and elevation). Another thing to remember, and this goes with most joint injuries, ice the area within the first 5 to 6 hours.

Afterward, apply heat. The cold keeps the swelling down, and the heat promotes blood flow and healing. An ice pack can be applied for no more than 20 minutes, and the same goes for the heat.

For most martial artists, this comes from hyperextending the knee during kicking drills or missing a target and by kicking improperly. Most of this can be alleviated by wearing a knee or ankle brace. I would highly recommend this as a tool to prevent long-term m damage. Another suggestion would be to annually get an x-ray and MRI of your legs every other year and once a year after 38 years old. An ounce of prevention is worth a pound of cure, or at least my coaches used to tell me.

Broken noses, jaws, and cracked orbital sockets can only be protected by wearing good headgear. If a fighter is hurt anywhere in the skull, they just must allow for the bones to heal. This is an area where you can't even do light sparring with punches, kicks, or have takedowns performed.

For strikers, the issues that normally last the longest and can end careers are ocular (in particular a retinal detachment), mandible (jaw), and dental. Just relax and let things heal. Tissue damage is a little different.

Getting a black eye, cauliflower ear, or abrasions back of the neck or face is different and varies in severity. Usually, with this, you just have to cover the area with some sort of protective equipment or possible gauze and tape. To prevent and minimize swelling, icing is highly recommended.

Damage to the small bones in the fingers and toes are common when training for striking and kicking. Depending on the severity of the injury, you may just need ice to keep the swelling down. However, for broken bones, splints, and slings until the fighter visits the doctor and gets an X-ray, which they should do as soon as possible. MRIs and CT scans should be recommended for persistent torso problems to make sure that there is no serious internal damage.

I promise you that if you know anyone who has competed as a fighter of any type for more than a year, they have sustained either injuries from training or combat, Two or three probably have or have had missing teeth, long-term vision, or cognitive issues as they have gotten older. A few have had a concussion or two during their active fighting years. It is imperative that these issues are examined and treated as close to the time of origin as possible.

With grappling, there are bruises and tears from the mat that occur around the ears (cauliflower ear), knees, instep, toes, and forearms. Bruises and scrapes, at first, appear minor but can lead to serious infections and are the most common long-term issues that grapplers have, next to muscular and lower back problems.

Speaking of back problems, for most fighters and athletes in general, next to the knees, the lower back is the longest lasting and most persistent issue that happens. Back and knee problems should be addressed immediately! Back and knee issues can spiral into long-term debilitating and quality of life diminishing concerns. As I mentioned earlier, the closer problems are caught and resolved to the point and time of origin, the better the prognosis will be for the athlete.

So far, all the injuries that we have talked about are ones that are predominantly acquired during training. A lot of them will also cross over to the time of fighting. These injuries happened during the fight mainly but could also become more complicated because of the fight.

Eyes, wrist, elbows, shoulders, knees, ankles, toes, and head, are all areas that have minor to major injuries during the fighting. I can't count the number of tournaments that I have been to, where I didn't see half, if not all, of these injuries, occurring.

For me, the two athletes that I think of the most when I think of eye injuries are Sugar Ray Leonard and Harold "Scorpion" Burrage. Both were great strikers, and both had suffered from detached retinas. A detached retina normally comes about because of a punch or kick to the face. In point tournaments, at the senior levels, shots to the head are sometimes permissible. They were in the old days.

Today this sort of injury is less prevalent but nevertheless just as serious. Surgery is almost always the remedy. The injury is normally not discovered or confirmed until after the fight is over. It is imperative that if a fighter complains of blurred vision or inability to see colors that they immediately see an MD or an ophthalmologist.

If a fighter has been hit hard enough to have a detached retina, they may also have a concussion. Both are serious, but this is the one that may not show up or be obvious immediately. Concussions come about because of traumatic force to the skull.

Possible signs of a concussion are being unconscious due to a head blow. Although a person does not have to have been unconscious to have had a concussion. I have seen it when a person suddenly starts speaking gibberish or loss of memory. Staggering or walking in an uncoordinated fashion can also be a sign of it. Being hit in the head with punches and kicks, even with headgear on, can be painful and lead to a loss of brain matter and capability.

If your fighter has any of these symptoms, have them see a doctor. If they persist, they must stop training until the symptoms have stopped for a month. You have probably heard the term punch drunk. It comes from taking too many shots, and they have accumulated over the years. Loss of memory, damage to the nerves, and grey matter are clearly not good things and have to be taken care of as soon as the issues appear.

As we have pointed out, all fighters of all types will get hurt and injured eventually. It's going to happen, but you should not be afraid of this. Your injury is nothing to fear. It is your initiation into the brotherhood of fighting.

It is a rite of passage for all who fight. An injury should never stop your training. It might slow it down slightly but never stop it completely.

You and your team must develop a way of working around your injuries.

Your mind set will be the most important part of this whole process. When you talk to YOUR team, and they are YOUR team, you must look at your injuries as being an opportunity to learn and develop resilience.

You and your team will look at not what you can't do but what you can do. My philosophy has always been, don't complain. Come to me with solutions, no complaints.

A great example of someone who came up with a solution to a problem was the great champion Mr. Bill "Super Foot" Wallace. In his early days, Mr. Wallace was a judoka. During a training session, if I remember correctly, he injured his right knee badly. While still in a cast, he began to study Shorin-Ryu karate.

Because of the cast, he was forced to train on his left leg with his kicks. This emphasis on his left leg paid off eventually. Although he became ambidextrous, he became so deadly accurate and powerful with his left leg that he became known as Super Foot. He overcame his injury. He made no excuses. He came up with a solution.

"Reject your sense of injury and the injury itself disappears." - Marcus Aurelius

This does not mean that you aren't smart about the injury or ignore it. Treat your injury with respect. While hurt and you are in recovery, don't re-injure yourself. Do not touch or irritate the area. Learn from this so that you can avoid it happening in the future. Make sure that you know how the injury happened in the first place so that you can avoid it happening in the future.

Chapter 19: Basic Skills for Fighting

If you do nothing else, always do your basics. For strikers, it's a jab, back fist, hook, and uppercut. Kickers have the roundhouse, sidekick, spinning back, and front kick (snap or stomp). Grapplers go for double and single-leg takedowns, hip throw, armbar, and rear choke. There are plenty of other techniques that you can learn, but these are bare-bones and should be practiced the most, especially on limited training hours.

Unfortunately, most people only train 8 to 10 hours a week. With this limited time, you must concentrate on the individual techniques and sparring. You might be able to add some very concentrated strength training in there, but just barely and only if you are about two to three months out away from the competition date.

"*Nothing in this world can take the place of Persistence. Talent will not; nothing is more common than unsuccessful people with talent. Genius will not; unrewarded genius is almost a proverb. Education will not; the world is full of educated derelicts. Persistence & Determination alone are Omnipotent!*" Press on – Calvin Coolidge, 30th President of the United States of America, 1923 - 1929

I still remember my first official fight. I was standing in front of this short, cute, innocent-looking blond and blue-eyed woman. She may have been in college or recently graduated, but it didn't matter to me.

She was not more than 23 years old. I was 13 but taller than she was. It was a Thursday evening class, which meant sparring. She was a brown belt, but that didn't matter to me. She was a GIRL (a grown woman), and she was facing a 13-year-old Black MAN (in reality, a little boy hoping and praying to grow into a Black man one day). She didn't have a chance. Luckily for her, I was feeling benevolent and had already decided to go easy on her.

She threw a few easily blocked punches. Of course, I blocked them all easily. She swept me. I gave her that one. She then hit me with a reverse punch right in the midsection. Lucky punch. I had been listening to our sensei and had been distracted. It wouldn't happen again.

It was time I showed her a lesson. Nothing fancy. I just had to show her that she was facing a real man. She tried a reverse punch again, and I moved out of the way this time and hit her with a backfist right on her rosy cheek.

That cheek was a little rosier than it was a minute ago. Oh yeah! That is how you do it! A few seconds later, I was on the ground and having my first experience with smelling salts. This was my introduction to sparring.

Sparring is what teaches you how to fight in the safest and most secure manner possible. You should wear as much protective equipment as you can at first. As soon as you can, and your instructor or coach says that it's okay, go to as little equipment as you can.

This is where reality hits you squarely in the eyes. Next to a real fight, sparring is where it is at for any fighter. Your sparring scenario should be close to reality-based as possible because this is where the rubber meets the road until you meet your first real opponent.

Timing, distance, power, speed, positioning, and everything else you need to win come from sparring. You learn to take a hit from sparring, and you learn to counter from sparring. Everything that you need to win you learn from sparring. You have to make yourself do it. Not your coach, instructor, parent, or partner. This is where it is all up to you.

The old Nike commercial is right. "*Just Do It!*"

More on strategy

The very first thing that you need to learn about fighting is that you cannot be lazy. You always have to be in the act of being in the moment. While you are in the ring, all of your senses have to be active and working at their maximum.

For this to happen, you have to work and train so that the only thing that your body has to do is react. Do not be a victim of what Mike Tyson said (I'm paraphrasing here), "Everybody has a strategy until they get punched in the mouth."

No practiced set moves, just scenarios, timing, and opportunity. If these components are in place, your strategy is the next thing leading you to that championship that you are training for. If your goal is to be a world champion or to dominate the local competition, you have to be willing to work and train harder than they do. For that to happen, you have to have a plan.

In war, you have to have three types of generals. One deals with politicians, money, and the public. In my opinion a necessary evil. Next up is your logistics or operational general. They are in charge of getting personnel from here to there and all of the supplies that they need to do their job.

Lastly, and in my opinion, most importantly, we have the field general. This is the person that is in the muck and mire. You get dirty, and they get dirty. I love this type of general because this is the type that gets wars won. Ninety percent of what they do is nothing more than a good strategy, and that is exactly how you want to fight.

The greatest boxer of all time, without a doubt, is Muhammad Ali. He was never the strongest, although he was strong. He was fast but not the fastest heavyweight. What he did better than anyone had a strategy in place. Most of the time, it started in the most subtle of ways, if Ali was ever that, before the fight.

No matter who you are, you should know that strategy is one of the most important parts of the competition. When you begin fighting, it's crucial, but most importantly, it is also when you really want to be the best that YOU can be. My main goal with this book is to make You are the BEST YOU that YOU CAN BE. Strategy is how you do that.

Remember, we all have two arms and two legs. We use these appendages almost identically the same way. Jab, cross, uppercut, and power punch for the strikers. Kickers, roundhouse, roundhouse, back or spinning kick with another roundhouse or sweep. Grapplers use a single or double with a mount and move into s submission of some sort.

These are all basic and bread and butter for fighters. What differentiates a basic fighter from the great fighter are the techniques or strategies that they use to get to the win.

All fighters have a strategy in mind to win a fight. They may not call it a strategy. They may say that they have a game plan, which is a strategy. A fighter saying that they are going to go in there just swinging is a game plan. Not a smart one, but it is a plan. Strategy uses intellect and guile to attain victory.

Part of your strategy has to be built around your talents, skillset, and fighting disposition. Are you a kicker, puncher, or grappler? Do you feel as if you like to attack, defend or counter? A counter fighter likes people to attack and then react. The belief is that if they are that close to attack that they are going to open up to an attack, and a kick or punch can take advantage of them.

An offensive fighter believes that they are stronger or faster and will overwhelm their opponent with their power, speed, and ferocity. Whichever one of these talents that you possess, you have to turn it into a strategy.

You should also remember that you are not a robot. Things happen when you are face to face with someone who is trying to knock your lights out. Stuff happens, and you must react in the best way that you know how to when the time comes.

This takes us back to training and conditioning. The more you train, the less you will have to think about what to do. Your body will just do it when it is time. This is going to sound awful, especially for someone who has a background in science and technology, but when you fight, stop thinking.

What? Stop thinking. As I've said already, you have to be in the moment when you fight. You can't think about what technique you are going to perform as you fight. It takes too long. That thinking stuff is for when you are in the dojo. In fact, the problem is not thinking but overthinking. You are going to think while you fight, but what you want to do is minimize your cerebral thinking and let the reptile brain take over.

This means that instinct and muscle memory are leading you. You think and analyses when you are training. When you fight, you act and react. You don't think about how you are going to act or react; you just do it. Be in the moment when you fight. Hear it, see it, feel it and be in it. The

Japanese call it Mushin no shin. Mind, no mind. This state of mind is important in combat and competition and is often overlooked, unfortunately.

If you have watched any sort of competitive fighting and seen where a fighter is completely out of gas where they can't fight anymore, this is where training comes into play. You watch them and just don't know how it is that they are still standing.

They are taking shot after shot, but they just don't fall. Out of nowhere, they throw a punch, kick or hold and in just a flash of a second, their hand is being raised in victory. Why? Because their training took over. They were pushed into survival mode, and those hours of training gained control, and they did what they had been trained to do.

Point tournaments are set up for the more aggressive-minded type of fighter. Most fighting is geared to the person who attacks. This is one of the complaints that is and has always been out there about competitive point fighting. Audiences, who, for the most part, are not composed of fighters or understand the shades of gray that are involved with fighting.

There are subtle nuances and gross spectacular actions that fighters have that are not perceived by the audiences that attend most matches. Because the masses view all fighting as a gladiatorial spectacle, they fail to appreciate slower, more defensive strategies. Because of this, the audience tends to like aggressive, showy fights and, i.e., fighters.

The promoters know this and unfortunately, so do the judges. They 8 out of 10 times want to award the flashier and more aggressive fighter because it excites the crowd more. Unfortunately, this goes against the ideas of self-defense which is the basis for most martial arts.

This is true across the fighting spectrum: point, boxing, Muay Thai, and mma style fighting. As a judge or referee at almost every single tournament that I have ever been to, I've been told that if it's a tie, the tiebreaker goes to the more aggressive fighter. In taekwondo and karate, they want you to give it to the person who has shown "superior" technique. The superior technique normally is defined as either flashy or aggressive.

Technique, however, really only works if you have a workable strategy when you are ready to fight. The following strategy will work only if you use it. Most of this is common sense. Some of it is counter-intuitive, but I have seen it work for offensive and counter-fighters.

The first thing you must learn is distance, placement, and timing. You must understand this and practice it over and over again. Let me explain what each of these is. Distance is how far you are from someone. Placement is how you are positioned in relationship to them. Timing is how long it takes to react to either an action or for your fist/kick to get from a to b. This is your fighting platform.

Are you a puncher, kicker, or grappler? For point fights, you only really need three good techniques to win. One is your scoring technique. The second is about showmanship, and the third is a statement maker. Some fighters have one technique that does all three things. Most do not. The veteran fighter does. They got that way to be practice, practice, practice, and more practice.

In order to score, you have to strike. Again, in order to score as things are designed now and for the foreseeable future, you have to strike your opponent with kicks, punches, or takedowns (takedowns are for black belts only, in most places in North America and Europe.) Next, the person that scores first has made the first impression. Referees like that person. The old saying is strike first and strikes fast. Striking first also gets rid of some of the fight jitters, so do it as soon as you can.

Punches and kicks should be thrown sparingly. Why? You don't want to get winded.

You keep throwing lots of techniques, and you get tired. In addition, your aim diminishes. What was thought of as a quick fight can turn into a battle if you are not mindful and take control of things.

To win at point fighting, you must decide if you are a kicker or a puncher. Grappling is a follow-up and helps on your endgame. Yes, I can hear my Judo and Jiu-Jitsu friends yelling and howling now. Yes, you can win a fight with your takedowns. Yes, you can win a fight with submissions. However, most fights are won through punches and kicks. Plain and simple – unless you are strictly MMA. From a fan standpoint, the excitement and fan appeal is from striking and kicking. This is where the mike is dropped.

To do this, several essential skills must be mastered for the elite point fighter. First, from the point of view of the puncher, the back fist and reverse punch have to be mastered and learned how to use from multiple points. Next, for the kicker, stamina, and flexibility to launch roundhouse, hook, and sidekicks are must capabilities. These are the weapons of the point fighters and ultimately of the future MMA fighter.

How these techniques are launched and from what angles will depend on the type of fighter that you are and the base style that you come from. Ultimately, it is your internal personal philosophy that will drive you forward.

Movement is important. One thing that you will see, especially on the larger stage, is competitors bouncing on their toes. Why? Because they are used to throwing lots of kicks and kicks in a row.

That and they have seen a lot of kickers do it, and no one has ever explained it to them. The bouncing keeps you up and the blood flowing. It prepares you to kick faster and higher up the body.

As a sidebar, you will see this more in Olympic-style Taekwondo than anywhere else. YouTube it, and you will see exactly what I mean. This can be a bad thing in tournaments that are what I would call real open tournaments. This means that there is a wider range of weapons used and ways for the opponents to throw them. If you are an old-school fighter or are trained by someone who was, you can see the difference.

If you are a counter fighter, this is easy. Your strategy with these sorts of fighters is grabbing them up close. The first time you do it, you grab with your forearms just below the elbow and middle of the forearm connecting and holding just above the opponent's elbow. If in the clinch, the referee will not see your hands locked. If he did, in most places, this would be an intentional stalling of the fight or a violation. The goal is to see how they respond.

If they get mad, better for you. It means that they have no control and should be easy pickings if you are a counter fighter. Right now, at the early onset, you are just looking for their response, along with the referees and judges. This will help you decide what will be your strategic response.

If the ref or the judges appear okay and you are a black belt, go for a hip or shoulder throw. Keep it controlled. Do not slam your opponent on the floor. Right now, you are testing the waters and seeing how tough your opponent is and what the ref will let you get away with.

If you cannot or do not want to clinch, the next move is staying outside of their range. Some fighters believe that you should always attack. If you don't attack, you are either weak or just not skilled enough. These are people who do not understand strategy. The unseasoned person will wonder what you are doing and let their guard down.

The experienced fighter will do the same thing and let you come in and then strike. If they are in taekwondo, they will ax kick or spin back/spin hook. If in karate, Kempo, or some version of a southern kung fu style, they will come with a lead leg hook kick or a reverse punch.

Sidekicks make statements, but roundhouses are faster. A roundhouse kick is like a jab for strikers. Just like boxing, when I use that front leg roundhouse, if the opponent wants to win, they have to escape my offense. What you are looking to find out is what you are comfortable with using as far as technique is concerned.

The next thing is YOU must know what those are before you go to your first tournament. If you are already fighting, you or someone around you should know what it is. Whatever it is, drill it over and over again until it is just automatic. The final thing to mention under the strategy is crowd control.

Crowd Control

No matter what type of fighting you compete in, you will have crowds. Point tournaments can have anywhere from two or three people praising your name to 1 - 2 hundred at some large ones. International TKD can have a little more than that at events like the Pan Am, European, All Africa, or Asian championships. MMA can be just like a point tournament depending on the venue, but up to a thousand or more folks in a major promotion. What is important for a fighter is to do two things, control the crowd or push them out.

For a point fighter controlling the crowd is a little easier than it would be for other types of competitors. Because the crowds are smaller, you can use "plants" in your audience. Plants are people who will look like they have no affiliation with you at all but, in reality, are there to be a booster for you.

They will usually be standing right in the middle of two corner judges. When you score, they go crazy and speak very loudly about how great of a kick or punch that was that you just threw. They also try to get the crowd screaming your praises.

The ideal number of plants is 6. Why 6? Six will allow you to plant someone on each corner and speak directly into each corner referee's ear. If they can get the name of the referee and say their name when talking, you automatically have an edge.

Never ever bad mouth or curse at a referee! First, it's just poor manners. Second, some referees will remember you or, worse yet, your team's fighter and start to nitpick or look to make bad calls. Even if you are right and ask for arbitration, which is allowed at most tournaments, especially open style tournaments, referees and judges talk. It doesn't take long for a bad reputation to spread. So, no matter how good you or your fighter is, it probably is not going to go your way.

Mental Acumen

No matter what style or method of fighting you participate in, the hardest part to master is the mental aspect. After this, it is the emotional component. The two together help you plan, strategize, and maintain motivation for fighting and competition of any type. Your mental edge provides you with the fuel you need for confidence.

This is really the easiest part of what we have here in this book. Getting your body physically ready is really simple. However, it does take time. You can't just step into a ring or dojo/school and be able to take a hit. For most fighters/competitors, it's their first few real punches or kicks that make or break the fight. It is the shock and pain of those first few blows that make a fighter/competitor give up or continue to fight. It's the same in real combat on the field of war.

"Pain is the best instructor, but no one wants to go to his class." General Choi Hong Hi – Founder of Oh Do Kwan and the International Tae Kwon Do Federation

Pain is something that comes with athletics and martial arts. Pain has two faces. One is mental, and the other is physical. Both can be adjusted to if not conquered outright. The very first thing to conquer is the thought of the physical pain to come. They say that it is all in your mind, and they are right.

I am a huge nerd. Outside of martial arts, I love science fiction the most! One of my favorite lines from any book is, *"I must not fear. Fear is the mind-killer. Fear is a little-death that brings total obliteration. I will face my fear. I will permit it to pass over me and through me. And when it has gone past, I will turn the inner eye to see its path. Where the fear has gone, there will be nothing. Only I will remain."*

Frank Herbert, Dune

Fear is our enemy. It's the thing that makes you give up before you have even get started. It is what keeps you from running that extra mile. Fear keeps you away from achieving your dreams. You have to overcome your fear. Fear is the first opponent that you must defeat. Once you do this, the other things fall into place. This is where your confidence begins to take root.

Confidence keeps you up. A confident competitor feels as if they can take on the world. Sometimes outsiders, people not part of the training cadre or family of the competitor, might think that the competitor is being cocky or overconfident. It should be this way. The fighter should expect this. In my opinion, they should use this as one of their weapons against their opponents. Let them think that the competitor is overconfident. Kings of the mental game are the great Muhammmud Ali and Conner McGregor.

"*If you even dream of beating me, you better wake up and apologize!*"

-Muhammad Ali

To help build your confidence, the competitor must have a goal. That can be beating a single opponent, weight division, grand championship, regional points, or simply having a "rep" in their fighting area. It doesn't matter what the goal is. What is important is that they have it firmly in their minds eye.

One tried, and true way of getting mentally ready for a fight is what you do before you fight. During this time, especially with beginners and under brown belts, you will see people warming up, stretching, and doing drills. This is exactly what should be happening. In most cases, colored belts, ages, and sizes start gathering together. This way, the promoter, parents, judges, and refs know who is going to fight and possibly what order they are going to do it in.

If you compete a lot, and in some areas, there are two or more tournaments a weekend. This means lots of opportunities for competition. Once everyone is together, and they start to pair folks off, have your competitor stand next to or right behind someone that you believe that they can beat.

Before this even begins, and literally as soon as you walk through the door, you should start to scout around and look for potential competitors for your fighter(s). Once dressed and in uniform, anyone that is there to fight should be warming up and stretching out. To fight, they have to be physically loose and ready. However, strategically you do not want everyone around to see your competitors doing it.

The reason why is that you want to see who you can beat! You are scanning for beginners, people you have beaten before, or those that just look like this might be the first fight they have ever had. Why do this? You want a fight or two that you can use to warm up with. Warming up with targets and kick pads are lackluster replacements to sparring with a human being.

Emotional

Next to the physical, the hardest thing to control is the emotional part of the competition. In fact, some people believe that in any form of competition is the most important part is the emotional part. The Love/Hate aspect is huge and energizes you a great deal when it's time for action. This is especially true when you are fighting against a particular school or opponent.

Every fighter comes across that one or two people that just brings the worst out in them. I had it, Muhammad Ali had Joe Frazier, McGregor had Diaz, and your sensei/coach/instructor had that one person that they just had to beat! We've all had it. You, the competitor, must find whatever it is that they don't like about that person and let that help them focus on how to beat them.

It doesn't matter why or how your dislike of the other person started. For our purposes, it is unimportant. What is important is that you are going to focus now on showing them that they should never mess with you. However, it should be pointed out that if you do this, you can only use it during training and not for the fight. Why? You make bad decisions when you are overly emotional.

If you are in a real fight, don't get mad at your opponent; get mad at yourself. Again, Why? Why? Because you did not train hard enough. You had the time to train and be prepared for the competition. It is the competitors' fight to win and lose.

I tell everyone I know, whether I train with them or not, to learn the poem If We Must Die by. My father taught it to me when I was too little to learn it and understand it really. Every competitor, no matter what sport, should learn it.

If We Must Die by Claude McKay

If we must die, let it not be like hogs

Hunted and penned in an inglorious spot,
While round us bark the mad and hungry dogs,
Making their mock at our accursèd lot.
If we must die, O let us nobly die,
So that our precious blood may not be shed
In vain; then even the monsters we defy
Shall be constrained to honor us though dead!
O kinsmen! we must meet the common foe!
Though far outnumbered let us show us brave,
And for their thousand blows deal one death-blow!
What though before us lies the open grave?
Like men we'll face the murderous, cowardly pack,
Pressed to the wall, dying, but fighting back!

Emotions, in my opinion, should only be used as a spark during the training session. This is not to say that you cannot allow it to push you in the fight. It can add a big spark to an engine that is low on energy, but as a whole it is better to have a game plan and allow that to help you conquer the opponent.

'Life is not easy for any of us. We must have perseverance and above all, confidence in ourselves.' - Marie Curie

Confidence and Perseverance

I realize that I have probably already gone over this, but confidence has to be there. When people are asking you do you have "it," they are essentially asking you if you have confidence. Confidence is that thing that separates you from others. I've seen fighters who were brave, but they were not confident.

My goal was to stop being bullied. I was a little kid. I knew I was strong, just not how strong. It took lots of training for me to find out just how physically and mentally strong I was.

I had to be obsessed with it. I thought about it all day, every day. I trained to make myself confident enough so that I could be confident enough to defend myself. I realize that it sounds strange. It must become an obsession for you so that you can become better.

"There is no talent here, this is hard work. This is an obsession. Talent does not exist, we are all equal as human beings. You could be anyone if you put in the time. You will reach the top, and that is that. I am not talented. I am obsessed." - *Conor McGregor*

A good fighter and warrior have one great thing in common. Persistence. Not necessarily in the ring or battlefield, but with a fighting spirit lit by a goal. When you train, you may dread going to the gym, but you go, and you do those drills until your limbs feel like they will fall off. You rest, and you do them again. You do reps, and you feel tired; you keep going. You spar, you get knocked down, you get back up and keep going.

We all face problems. Things happen that may at first appear to be unsurmountable. They can appear in different guises. Problems can be emotional, financial, or physical. They always happen when you least expect them, and they never happen when you are prepared for them.

When I was in high school, I had a girlfriend named Barbera Priestly. She was my first real love. I thought, mistakenly, that she was a little church mouse. She played cello and violin in the school's orchestra. She was a library aid. She didn't wear a lot of makeup or hang around rowdy people.

Before she met me (she was about 16 going on 17), she was told that she only had a few years to live. She told me that she was always scared about going to the hospital and never leaving. Did this stop her from enjoying life?   No. She jumped into everything that she did. We went to restaurants, museums, clubs, and she even came with me to spar. Every time she did something, she made sure that she had fun or learned something from it.

 If she didn't, no matter, she tried. The doctor's death sentence meant nothing. She is also the first person to show me what perseverance was. I was training for a wrestling match one time. I had lost my weight class two weeks prior. I was going to see the same guy again at the next match. I didn't want to work out. I felt sorry for myself.

She smacked me on the back of my head, grabbed me by my triceps, and dragged me to work out. She told coach Delmonico that I was a little girl, again, no insult to little girls and that he should kick my ass. Before I went into the training area, she told me to stop being a pussy and to pull my big boy pants up. I worked out hard for the next week, and I won. From that day on, I never gave up. Even if I had a loss, I kept going. That inspiration from her is still with me. I carry my big boy pants with me everywhere now.

The good thing is that sometimes there are examples of people who have overcome adversities and rejections that we have never heard of or thought were possible. Examples of failure and then success. Why? Perseverance. Here are just a few stories that you may not know about.

Walt Disney was considered a failure by almost everyone who worked with him and that he worked for when he started on his road to entrepreneurship. When he lived in Kansas City, he worked for the Kansas City Star. His boss told him that he was a failure.

He was fired because he, supposedly, lacked creativity. His first animation company was a bust.

He moved to California, where he failed again over and over. He was told that Mickey Mouse was an awful idea. Then it took off. Years later, he would buy the Kansas City Star.

Jack Canfield and Mark Victor wrote the book *"Chicken Soup for the Soul"*. The book spawned a series of books in the same vein. They applied to over 130 publishers and were rejected by them all over a period of years. Did they give up after the 3rd, 4th, or 120th rejection? No, they didn't! They kept going and eventually persevered. The series has sold over 500 million copies worldwide and continues to go strong today.

I like to eat. I love chicken. One of my favorite places for chicken is KFC, better known as Kentucky Fried Chicken. A lot of people don't realize it, but the guy in the ads is based on a real person. "Colonel" Harland David Sanders waited until he was nearly 60 before he started KFC. He had been selling his fried chicken for years, but it wasn't until then that he was serious. Sometimes he slept in the back of his car just so that he could be near a restaurant. He later sold KFC and made hundreds of millions of dollars from it.

The list goes on and on about people and how they have persevered over adversity. Anyone that has ever trained someone else to be an athlete of any sort understands how to build confidence. Confidence is the first step towards learning how to persevere. What does confidence mean?

It means that you know yourself, your capabilities, and your abilities and are comfortable in that knowledge. The first thing that you need to do when training someone is to show them how far that they had come from when they began.

I love the use of videotape. I use it to track the performance of my students. It is also a great way for them to see how they have advanced from one point to another. It shows them in a very concrete way how they have persevered. I had a student named Paul. Great kid with a warm heart and lots of smarts. Paul did not like sparring. When I met him, he was a green belt and had lost at every tournament that he had ever been to. When back at the gym, he would duck and try to hide on the two days that we did sparring.

We had a few kids, as every school does that were just like Paul. In fact, one of the problems that we saw was that all of our students just needed to train more and harder. In this modern age, this is not an uncommon thing.

Of course, this is hard in today's world, especially the new Covid-19 world; of course, this was pre-COVID-19. This was pre-Covid-19, however, and it was easier to come up with a possible solution. Our plan was a simple one. We offered summer school.

Well, not really summer school. It just coincided with school being out and summer starting. Paul's mother forced him to come for the entire summer. We expanded training to Sundays and Saturdays from June to September for those that could make it. For those four months, he only sparred a select group of people.

All bigger and more experienced than he was. The biggest difference between the regular classes during the week, which were an hour-long, and the weekend classes were that the classes were an additional two hours.

One hour of stretching and exercises, 1 hour of drills and conditioning, and the last hour was round-robin fighting, then 1 to 1 sparring. Once each month, we would go to a local tournament, I would pay for it, and the students would enter fighting.

Paul's first tournament in July, he lost, but he was very competitive. At the end of August, we went to another match, which was on a Sunday. On that Saturday before, I sat everyone down before we started training and looked at the videos I had of all of them.

When I do this, I like to show them how their punches, kicks, and sparring looks and point out where they need some work, but most importantly, how far they have come.

When we got to show Paul his, he perked up. He could see how he had gotten better. You could see it in his eyes. Paul won his first four fights in his division but came in 2nd in his division. He won first place at his next two tournaments in September. He did this through hard work and perseverance.

Physical

When you look at images of famous fighters, either statutes, paintings, or photographs, what do you see? You see someone who is fit. A fighter's body is not just healthy; it is strong and ready to take anything on. Those famous fighters only look that way because they put in the time in the gym.

Unfortunately, when you start off, you don't normally look this way.

To get in fighting shape start off with basics. Before we do that, it is imperative that you check with a doctor to make sure that you are at least healthy enough to start to get in shape. Yes, you have to be fit in order to get fitter. The doctor will check to see if your lungs, heart, joints, and other body parts are able to take a little strain. Once they give you the thumbs up, it's time to work out.

For fighters, the goal is to be strong and flexible enough to throw the techniques that you will have in your arsenal. To that end, you will stress the body so that it will start to change in order to manage the stress. Thus, the body gets stronger and fitter so that you can achieve your goals.

To get in fighting shape, we have three things: exercise, calisthenics, and sparring. You will work up your intensity on each of these overtimes. Your coach/instructor will monitor how much and when you should do each of these. This is important because before a fight, you do not want to have over-trained or peaked either to early or late.

The fighter should keep a logbook that will have weight, height, chest, waist, arm, thigh, and calf measurements. This will help to track your physical development. It is key that you monitor this.

Diet

This is a sticky subject. If you are an athlete of any type, you should be eating well. There is no excuse. A good diet leads to a healthy body. A healthy body leads to victory. However, what type of healthy body is the question. There is the combat Spartan body, which I personally prefer but takes absolute dedication.

There is the combat military body, this is the most adaptable in the modern world, but it is still hard to maintain. We have the bodybuilder body, super hard to maintain and not compatible with a point fighters' goals. Fit and ready to go, more in line with most athletic goals, and what a point fighter can achieve.

Diet has several purposes. The first and most important is to keep you healthy. The next reason is to keep you strong. The third is to help you attain a physical presence. That presence can be light or heavy. Everyone reading this book should have as a goal to be healthy all the time.

Everyone who reads this book should also want to attain the second purpose. Anybody who is anyone should want to be healthy and strong. Number three is really for supermodels and fighters. Why? Because, outside of them, no one has to gain or lose weight the way that they do.

My recommendation is that fighters should fight in the weight class that they normally weigh when they are in shape. I am in the minority when it comes to thinking this way, but I think it is for the best. This will be your fighting weight. Your fighting weight is where you feel healthy, loose, and comfortable.

This means that if you are between 175 or185 lbs. fight at middleweight and not at 155 for lightweight or on the other end of the spectrum, jump up to 205 lbs for a light heavyweight. Going up and down has a huge unhealthy impact on your body and your organs. Additionally, there are various studies that indicate that this is not good for your long-term health.

For a fighter, but especially for someone who is cutting weight to fight, there is the issue of timing your diet for efficiency. This is super important for the serious point fighter or the person who is thinking about mma. Two to three weeks out from your tournament is when everything must be fined tuned.

The following is the most important part of this diet section. Keep a food journal for the first few months. This will be key to any future gains or losses that you may have. You must write down everything that you put in your mouth and eat.

Everything that you drink. This includes water and even gum.

I would also recommend that you put down when you ate and where you were at when you did it. Why? There is a correlation with how much you gain or lose based on when and where you ate. If you eat two cheeseburgers 20 minutes before you go to bed, that might be the reason you cannot get to your fighting weight.

You must weigh yourself a total of 6 times a day for a few months. Twice morning, twice in the afternoon, and twice in the evening. Why? Because you are looking to see if your body is fluctuating at all. It's essential that you document this. This is especially important in the beginning because this will set the foundation for what you will be doing in the future. You must get it right in the beginning so that you don't have to go over it again once you have established yourself.

For power and weight loss, especially if you are going to a heavier weight class, you will eat before and after each training. There is no pop/soda/juice (no drinks with more than 18 mg of sugar per day), alcohol (beer and wine included), candy, processed food (this includes Quiznos/Subway), French fries, white sugar, no dressing on a salad, ketchup, barbeque sauce, mayonnaise, dairy and no type of sausage or bacon.

If you eat meat: skinless chicken, salmon, white fish, haddock, cod, tuna, beef (lean cuts only). Eat-in-season dark leafy green vegetables. Each plate of food should have dark, leafy, and green vegetables, some sort of beans, and quinoa or brown rice. I encourage you to play around with the diet.

In fact, it is a must because you don't want it to be something that you dread. There are plenty of foods that are healthy for you that you can pair with other things to create a delicious and health meal. Part of this will be how you season your foods. Make friends with a nutritionist and a cook. Introduce them to each other. Sit down with them to come up with a selection of options for you. Once you have done this, you can start meal prep.

Meal prepping will help you from cheating. You want to get to the point that all you have to do on any given day is reach into your refrigerator and grab a prepped container of food, heat it up, and enjoy. I recommend prepping at least three to five days in advance.

Food Prep Ideas

An average day should resemble the following:

Wake up:

oatmeal (steel cut) 1 boiled egg

run/hit gym/drills

Back home shower and breakfast

boiled skinless chicken/quinoa w/spinach/kale and bell peppers.

Go to work/school

Snack - some type of nuts, fruit, or salad (water

Lunch - tuna/salmon, spinach salad, fruit (if you can get a workout in

Go home change

Pre-workout meal or smoothie

Weights/drills/sparring (light or heavy ask coach/instructor)

Dinner

fish/chicken/beef/seitan-veggies- quinoa/brown rice - beans

A good trick to use for filling your plate is to ball up your fist; whatever you are eating should not be bigger than your fist. Another trick is if you are gaining weight, add two proteins to each meal. If you are losing weight, add an additional vegetable to your lunch and dinner and take away your second snack.

There are lots of diets on the market. Keto and Paleo are just two of them, and lots of people swear by them. However, I believe you don't necessarily have to go either of those routes. Often changing your eating habits really come down to lifestyle changes.

Nothing huge, but fine-tuning it to how you go about maneuvering your life. Every person is unique. We all have different food cultures and eat differently. Because of that, and of course, our bodies' unique metabolisms are different. My suggestion is always to eat cleanly, and this will serve you well. I want to add a few other things that I have seen and practiced that are not diets, but I would highly recommend that you use them.

Drink lots of water. What you don't use, your body will siphon off by making you urinate. Stay away from as much processed food and sugar as possible. I know I've said it before, but it bares repeating. If it is a fruit or vegetable and comes in a package that mother nature did not put in, you probably should not be eating it. This next one, I'm going to get letters and emails about I know, limit the number of fruits but increase the number of vegetables. The reason why is because fruits have sugar, and sugar leads to fat.

Sparring

For a fighter/competitor, nothing beats sparring outside of a championship fight. Your adrenaline is flowing. It's primal and very addictive. The act of sparring has several components to it. There are also several types of sparring. The first type is often called flow sparring.

Flow sparring isn't really fighting. It is what you do before you start to spar. I have also heard it called flow drills. In fact, the very first time I ever heard of it was when I wrestled in high school with coach Delmonico. Flow drills are very popular in the grappling arts. We will use it in three stages. Hand/kicking strikes, leg strikes than altogether. If you are in mma, you would just add grappling as a fourth.

Along with flow training, you must add combinations. Yes, it is only one punch or kicks that counts, but multiple attacking techniques increase your scoring opportunities. Your combinations should vary in height and angle. In point fighting, you are mostly in a bladed or side stance. Historically this is for self-defense reasons. However, I look at it as a platform to launch your attacks. In particular, your kicks.

This is the reason that for point fighting, I would recommend that you practice your kicks hard. In particular, your roundhouse (this is your jab and main point-getter), front kick (sets up other kicks), sidekick (made for stopping and checking opponent movements), and if you are a green belt up, spinning back and hook (both are good for counter-attacking). Brown and red belts should add ax kick (great for retreating opponent of someone dancing on rings edge) to that mix.

A key thing to learn is how to blitz. From every technique that you throw, you, as a point fighter, should be able to blitz from it. Remember, point fighting is like a game of tag. Tag is a game of speed and not power. The faster you can get from the line and to your opponent, the greater your chances of winning are.

Tournaments have the same basic rules and guidelines. Unfortunately, there is no one set that is universally adhered to. Luckily there are some general things that everyone will see. First line up. This impresses the judges and referees. It's similar to being at school. Come to the front of the class. Why? Teachers like it.

Every tournament has a certain number of people that will show up for your particular weight class. If you are an under belt (someone below black belt), you might also have a height class thrown in there.

At a minimum, the breakdown is normally by age, weight, sex, and height. There are minor variations of this, but they are usually based on rank or age. Don't worry about it. Spar, lose, and learn. All of us, eventually, lose.

It is inevitable. A loss, especially when you are either young or on a winning streak, is hard. You say to yourself, "how did this happen?" or "why did this happen?" Have I lost it? Am I a bum?' All of these questions will go to your head. You need to silence them all. Learn to be humble!

This is your transition time, or you might be at the end of your championship period. In either case, you should not worry about it. Keep moving and keep training. You are either in a transition period to being better or a transition to something else. Both are good. Your mental state must be ready for either time period. Neither is bad.

Chapter 20 - General Point Fighting Rules and Tips

I realize that I am probably repeating myself and have done so multiple times in writing this book. Not to beat a dog down, but most open tournaments have the same basic rules and guidelines. Most. However, there is no one set of rules that are universally adhered to. Luckily there are some general rules that everyone in North America and Europe follows. We will go into those here.

If any big-time point tournament honchos are reading this, please feel free to speak to your brethren and get your acts together. Put together a single standard that can be used everywhere. If the

IOC (International Olympic Committee) can do it, you can too!

Judges

Each weight class has a ring designated to it. If you have ever been to a tournament or fight of any type, you will probably notice that the big dogs, judges, and promoters all kind of look alike. Those that look like they've been doing this for a while all look like they are getting ready for a colonoscopy. There is a reason for that.

These much-maligned folks are usually judges. They have watched and participated in martial arts for years and have had to deal with parents, prima donna fighters, vendors, facilities managers, and a host of other people who has been nothing but a pain in their respective behinds. Dealing with all of them has created that permanent pre-colonoscopy look.

Judges are normally in one of two places. They can be in the corners of the fighting area (four corners, four judges). Sometimes, they are sitting at a table that can hold three to six people. The sixth judge usually watches a camera. The judge watching the camera is like the judge at a football game who watches the action that is in question and plays it back so that they can see if there was a kick, punch, or whatever it may be and if it was legitimate or not. Obviously, this happens at the more prestigious tournaments.

The job of the judge is, mainly, to assist the referee. If the referee is unable to make sound and clear decisions or just isn't sure, they have the four corner judges there to assist them. Each judge has a stick with a red flag on one end and a white on the other. When a fighter scores a point, the judge will turn the stick up, showing the color of the flag that corresponds to the fighter who scored.

Normally this is signified by the color white. Some judges will utilize whistles, hand gestures, or other methods to get the referees attention to call a scoring point or some other judgement.

Finally, judges also assist in the lineup of fighters to get them ready to enter the ring/fighting area. They will help in sorting the participants into height/weight pairings. Once they are sorted, the judges and referee will bow the fighters in and have them seated and ready to fight.

Referee

The job of the referee is to be impartial and fair when it is time to make calls on points, actions of fighters, and possible outcomes. They start and stop fights. They also examine quickly any and all questionable activity by fighters. They pause and continue fights. They also, gratefully, announce the winners of fights. For issues that are questionable or that they are unsure of, referees bring in judges for assistance.

General Tournament Terminology

Line – Point on the ground, where the competitor and opponent stand prepared to fight within the ring. This is usually two parallel lines taped or marked off within the center of the ring. They are usually 1 yard long and two inches wide.

Arbitrator – The arbitrator is the person who will adjudicate calls made by a center referee or ring judges. They will cover fighting and forms. They have the final say on all decisions that come before them. Most competitions will designate a senior ranked per person who has no students participating in the competition. Some places will have two. The reason for the second person is so that if there is a conflict, the second arbitrator will make the judgments.

Head Gear – This refers to the headwear that is usually made from polyurethane and covers the temple, top, and back of the head, and has a clasping strap that wraps under the chin. The point here is that the areas covered are usually point or targeted areas.

Safety Chop/Gloves – This safety equipment looks similar to boxing gloves except for being less bulky and that the palms are open and the fingers are visible. The most common colors are black and white, but blue and red are not uncommon. Pink pops up from time to time. String or Velcro strap secures gloves around the wrist, palm, and fingers.

Safety Kicks – This is safety equipment for the feet. It looks like a boot, and in fact, it is called a safety boot or just a boot in some locations. String or Velcro strap secures kicks around ankle, instep, the bottom of barefoot, or toes.

Ring/Center Judge (Referee) – This is the person who is of black belt or of comparable rank that stands in the middle of the ring right there with the fighters. They start and stop the fight. They are the tie breaker if the corner referees are even.

Corner Judge - These are the four people who are (normally) of senior rank or have demonstrated sufficient knowledge of fighting and competition.

The Ultimate Goal

The purpose of point tournaments is to demonstrate to your opponent and instructor/coach that by throwing punches and kicks (with the higher ranks, sometimes throws can be used at real old fashion tournaments) that in a real fight, you would be able to defeat an opponent. When the fight is over, the competitor with the most points and voted on by the ref and judges is the winner. While fighting, your job is to demonstrate skill, strategy, power, speed, and technique in just the right amount and way to show that you can kick booty in the street. Tournaments are a fun and safer way of doing just that. But....

The ultimate goal for any fighter is to kick the other person's butt. Anything else is superfluous. Anything else is also the opposite of why you learn to fight. Never lose sight of that.

The Fighters and What They Wear

Although most people don't notice it, as soon as the doors open, everyone is starting to put the competitors into their categories. There is an invisible bar code that is stamped on you as soon as you walk in or step to the register's desk. Starting with the promoters, referees, judges, and vendors and all the way to the parents and other competitors, everyone is putting you, the competitor, into a category.

Competitors are placed by weight, height, sex, and age in the point fight world. The organization that sponsors the tournament decides on what you wear and how much. The venue will also decide on the quality of the fighters.

The more prestigious, the better for the black belt or good fighters. There is a huge difference between fighting in the gym of Senn

High School on Chicago's Northside (no shade to my alma mater) and Paul Mitchell's annual tournament in Los Angeles. The type, quality, and ambitions of the competitors are vastly different.

The good thing is that what you wear and how you wear your equipment is universal. Historically, you were required to wear the traditional uniform of your style. This would be the mid-1970's and back. Starting in the late '70s and 80's we saw modifications to this. Some uniforms had bell-bottom pants with the top exposing the forearms and mid-drift of the fighter. Flags and other symbols were woven into the uniforms.

The uniforms became statements about who the fighter was and where they were from. For a while, it was just the superstars; then it was whole schools. Some were made out of silk, linen, and other more flamboyant materials. Fighters wanted to distinguish themselves from others, and so did schools and the various styles. After a decade or so, things started to calm down a little.

Some schools still require that, at least, younger, or brown belt and below, still wear a traditional gi/dubak or uniform that their style traditionally trains in. Normally they would be plain and without stripes or embroidery. Popular uniform colors are traditionally white, black, blue, red, or various combinations and shades of these colors.

Behind one of the fighters, their obi/belt/sash, they will have a red or white napkin or handkerchief looped through. The other fighter would have nothing. This is so that a judge or referee can clearly identify them. In the last few years, the more established tournaments will have red or blue gloves to differentiate the fighters. The WKA and other worldwide organizations have adopted this tactic.

Once it is time to fight, it is imperative that the competitors are prepped and ready to compete to the best of their abilities. A key factor is that they are safe from as much harm and damage as can be permitted to someone who has a goal of harming another human being, even if it is only theoretical.

The first thing that a referee is responsible for is asking the competitors if their equipment is on and fits appropriately. Next, they ask if they are aware of the rules and what they mean. Finally, they will go through a checklist of the equipment that is required for the event that they are competing in. This process is the same or similar in all combat arts from point, boxing to mma. There are only slight variations to this.

Below are the basic pieces of equipment needed for a tournament. The basics are a cup and mouthpiece. Then we add a foot, shin, and hand pads of some type. After that, we progress to headgear. We finish it all off with bodyguards of various styles. The following gives you an idea of what they all look like:

Cup/groin guards (there are also breast guards for women)

Mouthpiece

Foot, shin, and hand pads

Headgear

Possibly a bodyguard

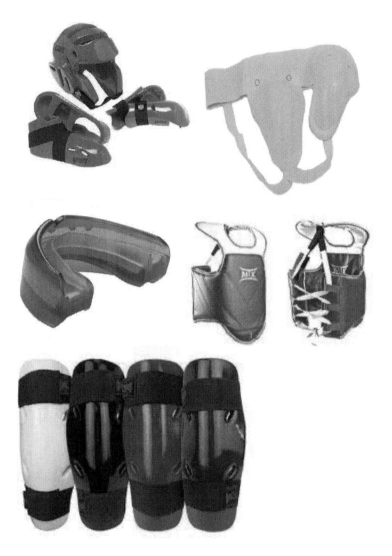

Target Areas and Points

Point tournament scoring can be simple. Point value varies from place to place and from style to style.

Taekwondo tournaments will give more points to kicks and their level of difficulty. Traditional kung fu fights will look for combinations and how close the fighters have come to actual harm without hurting someone.

It's always best to check with the promoter first as to what the point values are. Additionally, I think that it is best to check the website and download the rules and regulations before attending an event. Most sponsoring organizations provide this information on their respective websites.

It should be pointed out, and I find this interesting since most schools highlight the self-defensive nature of their systems; in my 40 plus years in the martial arts, I have never seen anyone given a point for a defensive technique. Points are only given for aggressive, forceful attacks. Nothing for a good defensive technique. I find this interesting since we are normally teaching people how to defend themselves and not how to attack someone.

In most cases, scoring is limited to the following areas of the opponent's body in point tournaments. This is done for safety reasons. When and how scoring is done is by rank and level of advancement:

- Head (top and side)
- Face (lower ranks - under brown or red belt are normally not allowed to touch face)
- Chest
- Abdomen
- Side
- Back
- Groin (usually only black belts)

Points are given not just for tagging, hitting, kicking, or throwing the opponent. The following are some of the subtleties that go into the process.:

- Superior technique
- Good form
- Good timing
- Accurate distance
- Awareness
- Sportsmanlike attitude

Winning: The second thing that it's all about

A typical fight is won by points that are approved by judges and referees through a simple process that sometimes looks more difficult than it is:

- By having more points than your opponent at the end of the fight.

- By extending a lead of eight points immediately ends the match

- If you render your opponent unable to carry on

- If your opponent is disqualified. (Excessive force or injury)

If the number of points is equal at the end, then the referee and the three or four judges consult and decide on a winner between them, or there is a sudden death fight where the first point scored wins.

Points

The standard setup is either on a hardwood or cushioned gymnasium floor or a matted marked-off at 8m x 8m with an additional 1m on all sides. During set up, allow for a two-yard buffer to existing all around each ring area. This is used for competitors to sit and wait for their match.

Once the referee and judges have taken their places, competitors should exchange bows to each other than to the referee and, in some cases, judges. The fight starts when the referee shouts begin in either Japanese/Korean/Chinese or English." Both fighters should attempt scoring techniques (punches, kicks, and throws) on their opponent.

If the referee indicates a point by first looking at each of the corner judges and looking to see if they saw a point scored. The more judges that agree with the center ref at what was scored leads to a point going to the fighter.

When the referee shouts YAME and the contestants, judges, and referee all resume their original positions. The judges will then indicate their opinion by means of a signal (usually by one of two flags colored red and white). If the score is to be awarded, the referee identifies the fighter and the area that they attacked and then awards them the relevant score and then restarts the bout by shouting " HAJIME!"

If one competitor establishes a clear lead on points during a match, then the referee can call a halt to the bout and declares them the winner.

If no competitor establishes a clear lead on points during the fight, then the fighter with the most points is declared the winner.

In the event of the points being, the referee and the judges will decide who is the winner of the bout or go for a tiebreaker by seeing who gets the next point first.

Fights can end earlier if one competitor is knocked down and is not in a position to carry on or if one fighter is disqualified.

And for our main event and in this corner......

You've trained, prepped, and are now ready to fight. Everything that you have done, from eating clean to weightlifting, conditioning to sparring, has all prepared you to fight. Tomorrow is it. What now?

You prepare for your big day a week in advance. I like writing lists and checking things off. If you make a list, make it simple and easy for you to use. I'm an anal detail guy, and on my list, I include everything from what color underwear I'm wearing that day to the type of cologne I'm wearing and what time I will put it on. If you are not like me, just write down the essentials and must-haves. Here is a sample of what I mean:

- Confirm date, time, and place of fight.

- Confirm that your coach, instructor, or parent will be there with you as your advocate.

- Confirm rules and guidelines no later than a week before. Make sure that you understand them and that your advocate has a copy of them.

- Confirm required equipment.

- Confirm transportation there and home.

- Pack uniform, equipment, and what you will clean yourself with after your win.

- Bring extra money to buy souvenirs and other items. (My equipment was stolen one time. Luckily, I had brought extra money and was able to get safety kicks and punches. I won that tournament).

The main event a.k.a. You fight

You either win, or you learn something new so that you can win the next time you fight. Every fight is a crapshoot. By training hard and long hours, you increase your chances of winning conclusively. As you fight more, your chances of winning increase. You also gain confidence. With confidence, you have more victories.

Hopefully, you have today and tomorrow off. Today (the day before the tournament), you relax and get everything ready for tomorrow. The very first thing you need to do is to relax. I realize that it is easier said than done, but this is important.

You must try and get as relaxed as you can. If this is your very first fight, this will almost totally be impossible, but I assure you that it can be done. If not, this was a sparring session that you paid for. You either win, or you learned a lesson. Both are good for you.

Your fight will happen. You will win. You will see another day. Just relax. Yes, it is very easy for me to say this, but you will survive fight day, and you will do this again. I promise you, even if you lose, your world will not stop spinning. Life will go on. You will live to fight another day.

Chapter 21 - MMA, Traditional Martial Arts, and the Future of Combat

Today, with so many things around to grab a person's attention, there is no wonder that attendance at traditional martial art schools is down. Most martial arts schools have small and inconsistent numbers of students. Except for Brazilian Jiu-Jitsu (BJJ) gyms and MMA schools. BJJ schools, which are very popular currently with males 16 - 42, make up the vast bulk of the martial arts schools that are profitable, and the market seems to be growing steadily. The same goes for MMA gyms.

At the time of writing this book, I did not have solid numbers, but I would imagine that there are three times more BJJ and MMA schools than there are for any other martial arts. This would be especially so if comparing it to Kung Fu and traditional karate such as Shotokan or Goju Ryu. Tae Kwon Do is still, in raw numbers, the most popular martial sport out there, and that is even compared to judo, the cousin of Jiu-Jitsu.

Registered participation in fighting schools is normally not that big. Even if you look younger than 16 years old and examine the normally core group of 8 - 15, the numbers appear to be down. Martial arts participation is primarily a male pastime. The number of female participants is small and rarely last as a lifetime activity as much as it does with males. The number of martial arts gyms that are owned and run by women in the United States is almost non-existent. Those that are around almost exclusively exist in very large cities.

As mentioned a moment ago, BJJ is probably the most popular combat sport outside of TKD. It is a very testosterone-driven endeavor.

Most classes at some of the bigger gyms/schools are almost exclusively male. Of those, 80% would probably be considered to be in very good shape when they arrived at their school. MMA and BJJ, in particular, can sometimes be a very "bro" type environment. Of course, this is not the case everywhere, but I always advise parents and students to look around and ask lots of questions before signing a contract or joining a gym.

Fighting is a combination of art, finesse, skill, intellect, and brutality. At every level, there is joy and pain, dominance and submission. To get to whatever is the top of your mountain, you must go through the pain of reaching that top. You reach that summit by battling others who are going that same path. Every day this is happening on a micro level, but it is also happening on a macro level with the martial arts school. More so with the traditional school.

What I view as the major difference between mma and traditional martial arts is the degree of feedback and practical response from the instructors. The other difference is the way that they are trained and why. Let's look at the feedback and response part of this first.

The best thing about a BJJ class is that there is a minimal ego that exists in the class. Students call their instructors by their first name or, in some cases, say professor or even coach. It is often a very relaxed atmosphere. For the first part of training, the instructor watches, then joins in and does the same thing. In many traditional martial arts, this does not happen.

In BJJ, the techniques are fewer in number but are practical and are worked on over and over. In many traditional schools, this is not the case. There are pre-arranged techniques that are designed to defend against someone who is in a forward stance and has their hand chambered and moves in a straight line. Of course, this is not realistic.

Karate, kung fu, and taekwondo schools must bring realism back to their training and practice real fighting. One major thing that has to be eliminated in my idea is kata or forms. Or at least eliminated from the way that it is practiced and trained now. This is where I eat the words that I have just written, or at least nibble on them somewhat.

In the age of Covid-19, I have found that kata can be helpful. After all, it is similar to shadow boxing. What I think should change is how kata is created and by who. Instructors, you should have your fighters create kata. Give them a set of scenarios for them to create it in and have them demonstrate it to you. As an added proof of concept, have them perform a bunkai.

Bunkai, if I remember correctly, means to break down. You take what is in a kata, and you break it down to its components. The way that I was taught is that you show what each move is with a partner. This way, it gives life to each movement. The viewer or audience is not just guessing what the fighter was doing; they see what they are doing.

If on the front of your studio or dojo you have that you teach self-defense, you are obliged to get rid of traditional kata/forms without bunkai also being taught. You can save it for people who want to become black belts or who are interested in total martial arts history. In fact, I believe that you should have three tracks in every traditional martial arts class.

Track 1 would be for those that want to be teachers and coaches. These are people who will become black belts in the traditional sense and continue the legacy. They are tested annually. They have to understand tracks 2 and 3. They are also responsible for writing at least 1 academic paper a year and taking part in training or practice for track 2 and 3 two days out of every week for five years (or whatever you consider to be a **thorough** time period) to be considered for promotion.

Track 2 would be for those that want to coach and or referee. These folks only train in striking and grappling for self-defense and competition. To attain the level of coach, they must have had at least 20 fights (it doesn't matter if they have won or lost) within a five-year period prior to being promoted to coach. They will have to have an understanding of techniques and their pros and cons, along with anatomy, emergency care, nutrition, calisthenics, and weight training.

Track 3 is for those who only want to fight. This track would have three belts. White, for beginners, of course, and those learning the basics. Purple is for those who have developed some skills and can perform at a high level of proficiency and have demonstrated it either through competition against others in open tournaments or has demonstrated technical proficiency in striking and grappling in front of black belt level practitioners within the style. Brown with a stripe is ready to compete or is ready for self-defense.

This last part does propose some ingenuity. In most military training, there is always a self-defense component. It is short and sweet. However, it can be very brutal. As an example, you have the official Marine Corps Martial Arts Program or MCMAP. It is just as rough and tough as you would imagine something that the Marines would put together. It is no-nonsense, no-frills, and no bs.

MCMAP was started back in 2001. It teaches Marines how to use all sorts of weapons, including weapons of opportunity, which I like a lot. The key thing is that it teaches close quarters and basic hand-to-hand fighting. In addition to this, MCMAP teaches team building, character development, and leadership skills. Their motto is "One Mind, Any Weapon." Why does this sound so familiar to you? It is exactly what most traditional martial arts strive to do. I think that the ancient Japanese Samurai and their Korean equivalent, the Hwarang, would be very comfortable and familiar with this.

Another similarity to traditional martial arts is that MCMAP has a belt ranking system. The colors of the belts are worn with a Marines standard combat utility uniform. There are five basic belt colors. The first is tan (akin to being a white belt 27.5 hours to complete). Grey belt is your second level and requires 25 additional hours to complete.

You train for another 25 hours, and you attain green belt status. At this rank, you are at the first instructor level and can not only teach but also promote someone up to the green belt. Next up, you have a brown belt which requires another 33 hours of training along with a recommendation from senior staff. This then brings us to the first of six blacks.

I mention all of this because I firmly believe that this is exactly how a traditional martial arts school used to be run and still could be. Historically, many martial arts schools were just like this. What's old is new again.

Right now, when you look across the martial arts landscape, you see Jiu-jitsu/MMA schools popping up all over the place. As a student of martial arts history and fighting, this looks familiar to me. We saw this same phenomenon back in the mid and late '70s with kung fu schools. They were everywhere.

The same thing happened in the '80s with fitness and health schools. What made them a little smarter was that they brought someone into their facilities that taught kung fu. Then there was the explosion of Tae Kwon Do schools with the talk of it possibly becoming an Olympic sport.

Suddenly there were kwans (kung fu schools) and dojangs (taekwondo schools) on every corner, and all of them were saying that they were the best and the ultimate in fighting. The traditional karate or judo school's enrollment plummeted. However, some schools survived by adapting. The good schools, with real traditional instructors that were successful, stayed afloat. Adaptation is what is needed. That's what must happen now.

Jiu-jitsu advocates claim that one of the reasons why they are so much more effective is because it is practical and more realistic. Of course, we know that it is not the ultimate fighting style, and the reason why we know that is because of the fighters that are in mma. I, however, do agree that you, as a fighter, should be as well-rounded as you can be.

If we look at "ultimate fighting" style fights, we will see that the sorts of people that originally went to and fought in these events were not high-end athletes that represented their styles at the competitive level that you saw represented by the Brazilian (Brazilian Jiu-Jitsu) athletes.

Why was this? In my opinion, you didn't have the same financial incentive to get a taekwondo or karate practitioner to fight in a mma tournament as you do now. For karate guys, the money was in full contact and kickboxing tournaments, not in mma.

Proof of this is available. Bill Wallace, Benny Urquidez, Don Wilson, Joe Lewis, and Howard Jackson were all top-shelf athletes and amazing fighters who could and would have been able to compete easily, in my opinion, against any BJJ fighter during the early ultimate fighter years. The difference is in the size and amount of the purses. As a side note, did you know, especially in the early days, a majority of your MMA referees come from a traditional martial arts background?

Mixed martial arts, in my opinion, is the precursor to point fighting. Not modern mma, but the idea of mma as it currently is formulated. Not to ruffle any feathers but the way that it looks now is a mirage that was created by an entertainment company co-opted by the Gracie family.

The Gracie family has a distinguished martial arts pedigree. The Gracie family should be proud of what they have done. They have saved martial arts and confirmed the idea that Bruce Lee had about a continuously growing and evolving fighting art. I, for one, wish to thank the Gracie family because, without them, we would not have the flourishing martial arts world that we currently have.

Jiu-jitsu came to Brazil directly from Japan. Let me correct that, they originally learned Jiu-jitsu by studying judo from the famous judoka Esai Maeda. If you look the name up, you will also see that he was also called Conde Koma. Not sure why that was. Mr. Maeda was a direct student of Jigoro Kano, the creator of judo. Judo is great but has a different emphasis than Jiu-jitsu. Also, Judo does not have the kicks and strikes, few as they are, that Jiu-jitsu has. What it does excel at is its throws and chokes.

I'm of an era that had guys fighting behind schools and who walked into dojos to challenge the top student, if not the head instructor, to do battle. Oddly enough, this is very similar to what the mma fighters do when they call someone out. The goal is to prove yourself and to get recognition. This was partly what we were doing back in my day.

MMA and point fighters are either looking to get up the pecking order and fight better fighters or to go for the belt and make the big money. However, if someone takes you up on that challenge, you must be ready to make a statement. You must be ready to show them, and the world, that you are no punk and that you mean business. MMA fighters do these two ways.

The first way that is entertaining but dangerous (and I hate it from the point of a teacher and former fighter) is that the fighter puts on a clinic. What I mean is that they show off different attacks and techniques that are either showy or that they do all of the time. They want to show these techniques off so badly that they will do them several times. In my opinion, this is dumb because ultimately, other fighters pick up on it.

YouTube, Snapchat, and all of the other video-based apps were not around forty years ago. Everyone has a camera on their phone and has it with them 24/7. Because of this, fighters have a hard time keeping videos of them away from potential competitors. This means that people can review how you fight and, like it is with poker, learn your "tells." If you do not know what a "tell" is, it is an idiosyncrasy that you may have or a way of telegraphing what technique you are about to perform.

This is a major problem for some fighters because, just as it is in soccer, American football, boxing, and a host of other sports, there is a video available for people to watch of you and analyze it.

If you are a top 20 mma fighter in your division, I promise you that everyone that you are going to fight for the next year has a file on you with "tape" and goes over it with their coach and team.

Their striking, grappling, kicking, and submissions coaches are all going over your moves and putting together a plan for diminishing or taking away any advantages that you may have. On the upside, this technology is also available to you too.

Most fights in mma, are a few months or a year away, which gives a fighter's team enough time to put together a plan of action. Even fights that are only a month out still give you time enough to come up with a plan to neutralize anything that you have been bragging about or using repeatedly. This is the reason you should close a fight out as soon as you can. Even if your opponent is analyzing you, his team is.

On the other hand, promoters are going to pressure you to draw the fight out. Even coaches and teams might tell you to take your time. Forget that. Get in and get out. The longer you are in there, the more chance you have of getting hurt. If you are an mma fighter, go for it and take your opponent out as soon as you can. For a point fighter, get as many points as you can and run the board on your competition.

There is a movie called *Glengarry Glen Ross*. The story is about these sales guys at a car dealership. I would suggest that you check it out if you can. It is not a fight movie, but it has some very valuable life lessons in it.

One of the lead characters is a real butt head, and he has this one thing he tells the sales folks who are not doing as well as he did when he was in their position. He tells them that they should all remember their ABCs. This stands for A.lways B.e C.losing the deal. Closing the deal in fighting is finishing the fight. I want you to remember your ABCs.

In a mma fight, if you are not knocking them out, you should be in the process of always submitting them. MMA is not a point competition. Take them out! From the moment that you hear that bell, your job is not to entertain the audience. Your job is to listen to LL Cool J's mom and knock them out! Get in and get out. Let the audience go home and play with their PlayStations, Nintendo's, or watch Russel Crow in "Gladiator" if they want to be entertained.

Before I close out this chapter, I want to thank Mr. Jim Arvantis, who is often called the modern father of Pankration. I do not know him personally, but I am a huge fan. I was inadvertently introduced to Mr. Arvantis through Black Belt magazine back in the 1970s. In fact, it was through an article about Mr. Arvantis that I first heard of a thing called mixed martial arts. He deserves a great deal of credit for keeping the flame alive and in the public arena when it comes to the modern world's acceptance of the idea of mma.

Chapter 22 – The Meaning of Life

Life is looked on as being a very complex thing. I don't think it is. I believe that it is essentially very simple. I don't want this to sound like the mystical gobbledygook that I hate, but some of that will be unavoidable. The complex part is the biological part of living. Life, luckily, is more than just biology.

The second part is easier because it involves having a purpose and a feeling of why you are here. Knowing, or at least have an idea, of what will give the time that you are here purpose and meaning. With purpose, there are goals to accomplish something. It doesn't matter what that something is, but it is uniquely yours, and no one else has it exactly the way you do. To be happy is to accomplish a goal that you probably didn't know that you have set for yourself.

Life is all about being happy. What makes you happy may not make me happy, and it is specific to you and who you are. Life and existence **are** simple for you when you clearly think about them, but when you try to explain it to others, it seems to them to be complex and strange. For you, however, it is easy and simple. Life and happiness are EASY, but only when you decide and accept what it means **for** you and **to** you. It only becomes complicated when you explain it to others, and they try to duplicate it.

Happiness is also something that you must fight for. Especially your own happiness. You must hold tight to it. Others will try to take it from you. You cannot allow for this to happen.

Sometimes people may not realize that they are taking your happiness from you. They may think that they are helping you, when in reality, they are stifling and squashing your joy. You may have to fight tooth and nail, but you must do it. Whatever brightness and light that you receive from your joy, you must hold on to it and keep it close to you. You deserve to be happy, and don't let anyone tell you otherwise.

I was very proud of myself when I was able to write down what it would take to make me happy. It was only a few short paragraphs, but it was a revelation for me. When I tried to express it to one of the smartest people that I have ever known, it just confused them.

How could this be confusing to them? Then I thought about it. This was what would make me happy, not them. This was my "ah-ha" moment. This was when I had the revelation about truth. Truth manifested itself when one thought about how it became real for the person that it was meant for!

Fighting is the same way. What works for me may not work for you. We are different people, and we climb the mountain top of adversity differently. We start our climb differently and reach it from different angles and at different times in our lives. This book will mean different things to different people at different times in their lives. However, the basics of success will remain the same and are universal.

If you have bought this book and are using it, you have likely found a purpose for yourself. You are now on the path towards some goal, and I am happy for you. This means that you have found a purpose and some type of meaning in your life. This also means that you are helping me achieve my goal of helping and making people, one at a time, happy, and I hope, better somehow. Doing this is one of my purposes in life and means I have achieved a goal that I've sought for many years.

When I started this book, I had stage 4 lung cancer and thought I would be dead in less than a year. It is now two years later. I am alive, and my cancer is in, for all purposes, remission. I should be dead. I still have lung cancer. I should be dead, yet I am not. Part of this is because of new technology and a new use of chemistry. Another part is because I had another idea and dream for myself. So, should you.

When I pledged Alpha Phi Alpha Fraternity Incorporated, one of the first things I learned was the poem Invictus. Oddly enough, it was my dad who had introduced me to the poem. This and "If We Must Die" by Claude McKay, should be recited by every black belt and instructor.

"Invictus"

BY WILLIAM ERNEST HENLEY

Out of the night that covers me,

Black as the pit from pole to pole,

I thank whatever gods may be

For my unconquerable soul.

In the fell clutch of circumstance

I have not winced nor cried aloud.

Under the bludgeonings of chance

My head is bloody, but unbowed.

Beyond this place of wrath and tears

Looms but the Horror of the shade,

And yet the menace of the years

Finds and shall find me unafraid.

It matters not how strait the gate,

How charged with punishments the scroll,

I am the master of my fate,

I am the captain of my soul."

My father, like my frat brothers, told me that
I could be a better person and conquer my fears if
I just had a more positive attitude about life and
my existence. The key was to take charge through
being determined and doing the tried-and-true
practice of hard work and remaining focused.
Fighters feel this and intuitively know it. The truly

elite fighters live this philosophy in all aspects of their lives.

For those of you striving to be elite point fighters or elite in any endeavor that you choose, I wish you nothing but the best. I finish this chapter by quoting two of my favorite science fiction characters.

Before I get to that, let me say that I love science fiction as much as I love martial arts. My first science fiction tv love was Star Trek. Two of the biggest cultural institutions that show up are the Vulcans and the Klingons. The Vulcans, personified by the character Mr. Spock, wanted everything to be logical.

The Vulcan's had an antithesis, the Klingons. The Klingons were emotional but admired duty and honor among all things. For them, their emotions were put to use in defining their sense of honor. The pre-eminent Klingon character was Mr. Worf from Star Trek the Next Generation.

Both have several memorable signature sayings. For Mr. Spock, there was, "Live Long and Prosper!" For Mr. Worf, it was "Qapla," which meant success. The other used by Mr. Worf and the Klingons was "Today is a good day to die"! All are attributes of both fighters and warriors.

Science fiction, at least for me, is always used as a metaphor for life. Star Trek, in my eyes, is all about stories of human life. Every day is a new opportunity for experiencing life at its best. I personally see myself as a Klingon warrior; I believe that today and every day is a "good day to die," but I want you to listen to our good friend Spock and "live long and prosper!"

"*Never backwards, always forward. Always*"

Pop – The TV show "Luke Cage"

Supplemental Information

The information here will update every new edition. If you buy the first version of this book, this is where you will start. I will put all of the newest, and hopefully, greatest information, to make you a better fighter. This will, hopefully, always be better than the online content, because here is where I will put the information that has been proven to be the best for fighters and has proven through my workouts with my students or from what I see at tournaments. Let me know what you think.

Sport Karate Websites and Organizations of Interest

NASKA (North American Sport Karate Association) - Home - NASKA • North American Sport Karate Association

AKA (American Karate Association) - Home - American Karate Association (akakarate.com)

ISKA (International Sport Karate and Kickboxing Association) - ISKA World Headquarters – International Sport Karate and Kickboxing Association, Worldwide Leaders in Sanctioning and Regulating Karate, Kickboxing, and MMA (iskaworldhq.com)

Sportmartialarts.com - Home - SportMartialArts.com

WKC (World Karate and Kickboxing Commission) - Home — WKC World

Weight Classes for MMA and Most Point Tournaments

Standard MMA Weight Classes (Men)

Weight class	Upper weight limit
Strawweight	115 lb (52.2 kg)
Flyweight	125 lb (56.7 kg)
Bantamweight	135 lb (61.2 kg)
Featherweight	145 lb (65.8 kg)
Lightweight	155 lb (70.3 kg)
Super lightweight	165 lb (74.8 kg)
Welterweight	170 lb (77.1 kg)
Super welterweight	175 lb (79.4 kg)
Middleweight	185 lb (83.9 kg)
Super middleweight	195 lb (88.5 kg)
Light heavyweight	205 lb (93.0 kg)
Cruiserweight	225 lb (102.1 kg)
Heavyweight	265 lb (120.2 kg)
Super Heavy	Unlimited Maximum

Point Scoring Weight Categories **(Used by NASKA Sparring Divisions 11/2/2018 as template)

Youth Sparring	Youth Sparring Open Weight	Youth Sparring Grands
9 & under Boys	11 & Under Boys	10-11 Boys Tall vs Short
10-11 Boys Taller	12-14 Boys	12-13 Boys Tall vs Short
10-11 Boys Shorter	15-17 Boys	14-15 Boys Tall vs Short
12-13 Boys Taller	11 & Under Girls	16-17 Boys Tall vs short
12-13 Boys Shorter	12-14 Girls	10-11 Girls Tall vs Short
14-15 Boys Taller	15-17 Girls	12-13 Girls Tall vs Short
14-15 Boys Shorter		14-15 Girls Tall vs Short
16-17 Boys Taller		16-17 Girls Tall vs Short
16-17 Boys Shorter		
9 & under Girls		
10-11 Girls Shorter		
10-11 Girls Taller		
12-13 Girls Shorter		
12-13 Girls Taller		
14-15 Girls Shorter		
14-15 Girls Taller		
16-17 Girls Shorter		
16-17 Girls Taller		

Terminology

Japanese Terminology

Hajime - Start or begin

Yame - Finish or stop

Obi - belt in Japanese styles

Oss - Greeting or respect or acknowledgment

Dojo - Training hall or school

Sensei - Instructor

O-sensei - Head instructor

Gi - Workout uniform

Kumite - sparring

Rei - Bow

Mawatte - Turn

Khon - Basic tech

Kamae-te - Move to ready position

Dachi - Stances

Uke - Blocks

Tsuki - Punches

Geri - Kicks

Kata - pre-arranged form or movement

Chudan - Middle

Dozo - Please

Karate-ka

Migi - Right

Hidari - Left

Sempai - Senior student

Kiai - Shout

Keage - Snap

Barai - Sweep

Domo Arigato - Thank you (say it when speaking to senior or person of honor.

Domo - Thank you (say when speaking to junior or person of lesser rank

Nage - Throw

Nodo - Throat

Jodan - High or upper level

Hai - Yes

Anata - You

Embusen - Where a kata begins or starts

Harau - Sweeping technique

Mae - Front

Mo Ichi Do - Do it again

Te - Hand

Yoko - Side

Seiza - Kneel

Yoi - Ready

Gedan – Low

Korean Terminology

Charyut - Attention

Dwi - Back

Sijak - Begin

Ti - Belt

Kyungnet - Bow

Kaesok - Continue

Pihagi - Escape or evade

Joomock - Fist

Baal - Foot

Balnal - Foot

Apchuk - Ball of foot

Balnal - Foot edge

Baldeung - Instep

Poomse - Forms or pre-arranged movement

Ap - Front

Kyoung ye - Bow

Kalyeo - Stop or break

Gu mahn - Stop

Barro - Return to previous position

Japgi - Grab

Son - Hand

Mori - Head

Anyeong Haseyo - Hello

Sabomnim - Teacher or coach

Ttwigi - Jump

Chagi - Kick

Dari - Leg

Mog - Neck

Milgi - Push

Dojang - School or gym

Yeop - Side

Kyorugei - Sparring

Jeonggangi - Shin

Hosinsool - Self-defense

Joo Sim - Referee

Joon Bi - Ready

Seogi - Stance

Kalyeo - Stop

Chigi - Strike

Kamsa Hanae Da - Thank you

Dobok - Workout uniform

Kihap - Yell for power

Kwanjangnim - Master instructor (5th degree or higer in WT)

Jeon - A round in competition

Jeum - A point in competition

Shi gan - Time out in competition

Jo sim - Referee

Bu sim - Judge

Kae sim - Time

Ki rohk - Recorder

Dorra - About face

Major Martial Arts Styles

Some of the places of origin are in dispute but are listed here because of lack of scholastic or solid historical proof. The names of the founders of various arts are also a matter of contention with certain arts for the same reason.

Aikido - Japan. Morihei Ueshiba, December 14, 1883 – April 26, 1969

Aikijutsu - Japan. Goto Tamauemon Tadayoshi (1677-1736) to be more precise he re-introduced Daito Ryu Aikijutsu specifically.

Brazillian Jiu Jitsu - Brazil via Japan, Helio Gracie

Capoeira - From Brazil, but an argument can be made for Africa and in particular western Africa. No founder and is practiced in Brazil and small parts of North America. There are pockets practicing in Europe

Eskrima (a.k.a. kali and arnis) – Philippines / It goes back to at least the late 1400's and early 1500's. Pre-colonization by Spanish

Goju Ryu - Japan. Chojun Miyagi (1888-1953), the founder of Goju-Ryu Karate

Hapkido - Korea. Choi Yong-sool November 9, 1904 – June 15, 1986

Judo - Japan. Jigoro Kano October 28, 1860 – 4 May 1938

Jiu Jitsu – Japan. Hisamori Tenenuchi before 1532

Kempo – Japan/China – There are various flavors of this style with no one clear founder of the ancient version

Kuk Sool Won - Korea. In Hyuk Suh August? 1939 -?

Kyokushin – Japan Mas Oyama June 4, 1922 -
April 26, 1994

Shotokan - Japan. Gichin Funakoshi is its founder.
It is practiced worldwide but more popular in the
Americas, Europe and southern Africa.

Taekwondo - Korea. General Choi Hong Hi
November 9, 1918 – 15 June 2002

Famous Martial Arts Entertainers

The following is a list of entertainers who are also accomplished martial artist. A few of them have studied multiple styles. In some cases I have listed their primary style and others what they may have studied later in life.

Dolph Lundgren (karate)

Jean-Claude Van Damme (Karate) - Wesley Snipes (Karate) - Jason Statham (karate)

Billy Blanks (Taekwondo) - Michael Jai White (karate) - Tony Jaa (muay thai/muay boaran)

Ronda Rousey (judo) - Danny Trejo (Boxing) - Katheryn Winnick (taekwondo)

Gina Carano (muay thai) Ryan Phillippe (taekwondo) Bas Rutten(karate/pancrantion)

Jeff Wincott (taekwondo/karate), Channing Tatum (kung fu), Taylor Lautner (karate)

Adrian Paul (karate) Ray Park(taekwondo) - Ho-Sung Pak (taekwondo)

Tanit Phoenix Copley (karate) - Vincent Cassel (capoeira) - Matt Mullins (shorei-ryu)

Karen Sheperd (karate) - Christine Rodriguez (kenpo) - Zara Phythian (taekwondo)

Hector Echavarria (judo/jiujitsu) - Michelle Yeoh (Wu Shu), Kristanna Loken (krav maga)

Brenda Song (taekwondo) - Lucy Liu (kali-escrima-silat) -

Victoria Pratt (kickboxing) - Athena Massey (krav maga) - Diana Lee (jeet kune do/escrima) – Dan Inosanto (escrima/jeet kun do), Summer Glau (kung fu)

Bradley James Allan (karate/wu shu) - Nia Peeples (kempo/wu shu)

Kelly Hu (kung fu/wu shu) - Will Yun Lee (taekwondo) - Bo Svenson (judo)

Ed O'Niel (jiu jitsiu) – Guy Ritchie (jiu jitsu) Willie Nelson (gong kwan yu sool)

Diet Ideas: Pre-workout meals

Fighters, like runners, need to be ready to go. To do that you have to do, you must get fuel in the tank. We have all seen fighters peter out in a fight. There are two reasons for that, one is bad cardio and the other is poor diet. Cardio is part of your training before the fight and just has to be there. Diet before the fight can be controlled up to the last few hours.

I am a former soldier and one thing that the Army teaches you is that you train the way you are going to fight. Your exercises and process are the same or supportive of it. You spar the way you are going to fight and so should eat the way that you will eat before you go into combat.

So that you do not get fat, you have to be in a caloric deficit. This means that the number of calories that you are taking in should be less than the energy output that you have. For example, if I am lifting weights, I have to lift for 30 to 45 minutes an amount of weight that challenges me. On average you should lift about 80% to 100% of your body weight. You will burn at least 700 to 750 calories this way. The more muscle you attain, the higher your metabolism rate will be, even when at rest.

Apart from vitamin D/C, I am not a fan of taking in extra supplements. If a fighter is eating a healthy and clean nutritious meal, they do not have to really take supplements, however, there are a few exceptions. I am a big proponent of drinking beetroot and pomegranate juices. Why? Because they are natural vasodilators. Vasodilators help in recovery time, increased ability to train harder, aerobic energy production and overall training capacity. Outside of this, eat clean. Balance carbs, fats and proteins.

Good luck in all of your training. May you find the path to happiness and meaning to your life!

Books That Should Be on Your Bookshelf

I realize that many people do not read books, but I am enamored of them and highly recommend that you buy and read some of the ones that I am recommending. If you are a nerd of fighting, a person that would like to be a champion, a person who just would like to understand what it really all of the components are of fighting, this list will take you there, or so I hope. Without further ado:

1. Make Your Bed: Little Things That Can Change Your Life...And Maybe the World
By William H. McRaven

2. Martial Arts for the Mature Athlete – A Guide to Injury Prevention and Treatment
By Dr. John T. Hippen, M.D.

3. Mixed Martial Arts Fighting Techniques – Apply The Modern Training Methods Used By MMA Pros!

By Danny Indio

4. Moms and Dads' Guide to Martial Arts for Kids – Karate, Judo, Taekwondo, and Six other Sports Rules, Vocabulary and Techniques. How to help out at home

By Coles Notes

5. Beyond Kicking – A Complete Guide to Stretching and Kicking

By Jean Frenette

6. Sport Karate Point Sparring – An Essential Guide to The Point Fighting Method

By Ed Yuncza

7. Training for Warriors – The Ultimate Mixed Martial Arts Workout

By Martin Rooney

8. The Science of Martial Arts Training Mixed Martial Arts Fighting Techniques – Apply the Modern Training Methods Used By MMA Pros!

By Charles Il Staley MSS

9. Comprehensive Asian Fighting Arts

By Donn Draeger and Robert W. Smith

10. Fight Like A Physicist

By Jason Thalken, PhD

11. The Anatomy of Martial Arts

By Dr. Norman Link and Lily Chou

12. Speed – Training for Combat, Boxing, Martial Arts and MMA

By J. Barnes

Thank you for buying this book!!

There are way to many people for me to thank who contributed directly or indirectly to me writing this book, but a few names really stick out. First of course are my father and mother, Joseph and Alberta Prewitt. My maternal and paternal grand parents Elzie and Jerlene Winters/John and Allie Prewitt. My wife Annette and daughter Alexis. All my uncles, aunts and cousins (Eric, Alexander, Sidney and Barbara Anne who are no longer with us) Brian and Hyacinth Caswell and the Ray man. Willamae and Albert Johnson, Lincoln University (PT-13) alumni and staff, Temple University, DePaul University, the owners of Superior Companies in Roselle Illinois. Every girl friend who put up with me training instead of taking them out on a real date.

I also want to include Sam Abdullatif, Joseph Riser, Matt Kusek, Mr. Raymond Johnson (my cool cousin and a second thank you), Debora Beverly, Gregg Lisatinski, Keith Reed, Excell Williams, Pastor Perry Archie, Alvin Davis, Leon Sutton, General Dr. Roosevelt Allen, Tory

Bryant, Benjamin Qaadir Shamballa (Benny), Roy Stamps, Lisette Laboy and Jay Green who all read various parts of the book and gave me invaluable feedback.

Finally, none of this would have been possible if not for the people who took time to train me and answer my millions of questions. I've had many instructors but here is a short list of some of the best: sensei Mike Revis, master Harold "Scorpion" Burrage (everyone at S.O.C.K.), master Anthony "Mongoose" Gipson, master Michonne Berry, master Cricket, master Shawn Gary, master Dominic Kim, master Choi, master Ben Peacock, sensei Gordon, (he still holds the record for hitting me harder than anyone has in my entire life – twice!!), sensei Mitchel, sensei Chopper, the Metcalf family, grand master James "Jimmy" Jones, (Sgt) Thorne, sabunim Eric, the Kung Fu Duks, Dr. Rajendran and her son, Ron Amundson, Ko Neko Dojo, grandmasters Preston and Otis Baker, Mr. Michael Cribbs and Mr. (Coach) Marcus Clarke who all either trained me or made sure I went to train. Lastly, my uncle Elzie "Billy" Winters Jr. who set me on the road to this life.

May you find happiness and meaning in whatever you do.

Made in the USA
Monee, IL
22 January 2022